MW01241868

THE WORLD'S MOST WELL-KNOWN STRANGER

A BOOK ABOUT THE HOLY SPIRIT

To Jan,
A True fellow Soldier.
Keep Fighting The Good Fight!
Love You !
Dan
July 2018

DAN ROBINSON

innovo
PUBLISHING

Published by Innovo Publishing, LLC
www.innovopublishing.com
1-888-546-2111

Providing Full-Service Publishing Services for Christian Authors, Artists & Ministries:
Books, eBooks, Audiobooks, Music & Film

THE WORLD'S MOST WELL-KNOWN STRANGER
A Book About the Holy Spirit

ISBN: 978-1-61314-390-2

Cover Design & Interior Layout: Innovo Publishing, LLC

Printed in the United States of America
U.S. Printing History
First Edition: 2018

In Memory Of

Stephen M. Dunn

I became Steve's stepfather in 2007. Our relationship—always good—deepened as we worked on my writing projects. *Lord, The One You Love Is Sick* was published in 2006. Steve designed the incredible cover for the book. Likewise, he read some of the earliest chapters for the book you now hold and was already thinking of just the right cover. On April 13, 2015, Steve went home to heaven. There he joined his older brother, Ronnie Jr., and his dad, Ron Dunn—a Bible teacher par excellence. I miss Steve and will always wonder what sort of book cover he might have created.

DEDICATION

Bob and Mary Robinson
My parents whose stories of the ways and works of God made
me hungry.

The Pastor's Wife
It takes a courageous woman to marry a pastor. Kaye has
done that twice now (I doubt if she will do it a third time!). She has
always maintained that her role was to pray for me; so she has and
does. The completion of this book is in no small way attributable
to her prayers. Often, I would read to her something I had just
written. In my excitement, I would read rather fast. After so many
times of Kaye pleading with me to slow down, she finally said
(around chapter eight), "I will just have to wait and read it when
you are finished." Well, here it is: written by the pastor, prayed over
by the pastor's wife. Read it as slowly as you wish!
Thank you, Kaye, and as you know, I am still falling for you.

Charis, Zach, and Seth
My one mighty daughter and two mighty sons, who, like their
mother and David's mighty men, always surrounded me, defended
me, and kept me going (2 Samuel 16:6, 23:16).

Kim
My one and only stepdaughter, who never got tired of seeing
me! Kim went to be with the Lord just as this book was entering
the final phase of publication. She was loved, and I will miss her.

The Lord's Sheep Under My Care
Who gave me space and grace to write, asked questions
regarding my progress, and who were happy to play their role in
helping me.

Molly McKim and Mona Humphrey
Who not only typed my long manuscripts but have done so
with a gracious spirit.

Acknowledgements

My sincere thanks to Dr. Bart Dahmer, Founder and CEO of Innovo Publishing. His confidence in this project and approachability when discussing it has been a great encouragement to me. And thanks to Rachael Carrington, Editor and Project Manager at Innovo, for her capable and helpful suggestions in smoothing out the text, even in the midst of multiple rewrites.

ENDORSEMENTS

"This book will help to fill a great need in knowing more about the Holy Spirit. It does a superb job of making this important subject clear and informative. A comment in the preface is very outstanding. It reads, 'One may know accurate theological information about the Holy Spirit and yet not really know Him.' Two of the outstanding themes in this book are brokenness and intimacy with God, which represents the work of the Holy Spirit so well. What a joy it was to read this book. The space of time in which we live can be properly called The Age of the Holy Spirit; so we should be very knowledgeable of Him and His ministry. This book will be a tremendous help in doing so."
—**Rev. Paul A. Travis, Field Staff of Freedom in Christ International**

"I came to know Dan Robinson through his marriage to Kaye, and I love his heart for prayer and walking in the Spirit. Our stores and shelves are filled with books on methods and programs and strategies. However, Dan's book takes us back to square one: the power of the Spirit. In these pages, you'll become intimately acquainted with the Holy Spirit, His ways, and His purpose. This book is a valuable resource in plugging back into the source and recognizing that He alone is our sufficiency in life and ministry."
—**Michael Catt, Senior Pastor, Sherwood Baptist Church**

"It is with pleasure that I endorse *The World's Most Well-Known Stranger*, authored by my friend and brother, Dan Robinson. The title might well have been written by an old Puritan writer who, way back in his day, said that the Holy Spirit was the least known, least loved, and least worshiped of the Trinity. Sadly, the same condition seems to exist in our day. This not an Ivory Tower treatise on the Third Person of the Trinity, but one that comes out of years of walking with, and learning from, the one who was sent to lead us into all truth. Dan speaks to the heart of the Paraclete's mission—to point us to our Savior. *When the Holy Spirit is given the floor, He will point to Jesus.*' Always! Thank you, Dan, for this reminder."
—**Ron Owens, Musician/Author, Ft. Worth, Texas**

"Dan Robinson has certainly written a thought-provoking work on the Holy Spirit, whom he believes is the world's most well-known stranger. He contrasts the knowing of truths about Him to knowing the Spirit as a Person, a Presence, and a Power. He goes on to point out that tongues in the book of Acts was God's method for evangelism—and not the message itself, but the Spirit always pointing to Jesus. He further underscores that to know Jesus Christ carries with it the privilege of sharing Him, and the Holy Spirit is the power for doing so. This calls for brokenness of the self-life, as resurrection power only and always follows Calvary death! Another encouraging emphasis is the place of the Spirit in prayer, as we add our prayers to the prayer of Jesus (Hebrews 7:25), and as the Holy Spirit already prays for us (Romans 8:26-27). One of my favorite chapters deals with intimacy. The author states, 'God has no favorites, but He does have intimates!' Then there is the deeply challenging matter of suffering and its relationship with the Holy Spirit. Surely there may be no participation in the life of Christ apart from our participation in His death! Finally, Dr. Robinson asks, 'Now what; so what?' It really does matter what we do with what we hear! We are accountable for what we do with God's Truth!"

—Jon Moore, Revivalist, Ft. Worth, Texas

"Full of fresh insight and illumination, this is such a helpful book on the Holy Spirit for both the new Christian and the more mature believer. For the new Christian, it leads them biblically through the scriptures, unveiling the truths about the Holy Spirit that sadly are not heard as much from our pulpits today as they should be. For the mature believer, time and the pressures of modern life have often dulled and eroded our original understanding and experience of the Holy Spirit. This is a book that takes you back to the fundamental teaching on this vitally important subject. Dan Robinson, calling on his own experience and study of the scriptures, seeks, in a fresh and personal way, to re-introduce you to the essential nature and work of the Holy Spirit. Read this book and be refreshed and inspired as you see God still at work, through His Holy Spirit, revealing more and more to you of our Lord Jesus Christ in your life and daily walk with Him."

—Philip B. South, Founder & CEO of World Action Ministries UK

"Dan Robinson has been my professor, pastor/mentor, and my friend for twenty years. It's a joy to learn and serve in the trenches alongside him. This book is not only a reflection of Dan's journey of knowing God (Father, Son, and Holy Spirit), it is also a manual

for the Christ follower to know the Holy Spirit and His mission. As you read with your eyes, I encourage you to listen with your soul!"
—Ted Edwards, Southeast Valor Coach for Cru and USMC Veteran

"Dan has drawn from personal experience and years of study on the important topic of the Holy Spirit. You will find this to be a very thorough and refreshing book that will encourage your personal faith in a practical way. In this book, you will receive more than just knowledge and inspiration but also a basis for a life-changing attitude in your personal relationship with God. This is so needed today for Christians to stay strong in the faith."
—Jerry Hyder, Associate Pastor, First Baptist Church, Sevierville, Tennessee

"In his work, *The World's Most Well-Known Stranger*, Dan Robinson has done an excellent job of taking his readers on a journey to understanding the purpose, presence, and power of the Holy Spirit. At a time when the influence of the church is being marginalized, and her voice of authority is diminishing in society, Dan writes with keen insight of something that is missing today that was actively present in the first-century church: the fire, the force, and the fruit of the Spirit. Dan wisely points out the clear signs and evidence that should be seen when the fullness of the Spirit is at work: clarity, conviction, conversion, and change. Dan has written this piece with a good balance of scholarly wisdom and down-to-earth practical usefulness. I highly recommend *The World's Most Well-Known Stranger* to both those that are new in the faith as well as those that are the most seasoned of disciples. Job well done, Dan!"
—Alan Stewart, Senior Pastor, Rechoboth Baptist Church, Soddy Daisy, Tennessee

"Each generation, it seems, is in desperate need of an authentic reintroduction to the person and work of the Holy Spirit. With the current proliferation of voices speaking to this issue, Dan Robinson's *The World's Most Well-Known Stranger* arrives at a crucial time. Robinson takes us straight to the Word of God where the Spirit introduces Himself, clearly, cogently, and with convicting power. With its conversational tone, careful exegesis, and easy-to-follow unfolding of truth, Robinson's book will become a timeless and helpful addition to both your library and your life."
—Tom Elliff, President Emeritus, International Mission Board, Southern Baptist Convention

CONTENTS

PREFACE

What if you knew nothing about the Holy Spirit? What if indeed He were a stranger to you? If we were at all interested in knowing Him, then we would pursue some avenue that would promise insight into Him. Maybe there's a person who knows Him; or maybe someone has written something about Him; or maybe even He Himself has written a book. All of these possibilities might enter our minds, and all of these possibilities surely would render insight into the Person of the Holy Spirit.

Yet of these three sources, it is the last one that is not only most reliable but completely so. The book that the Holy Spirit wrote is the Bible. He Himself has said so: "All Scripture is God-breathed" (2 Timothy 3:16). This means that the content of the Bible is the very exhaling of God, His very breath—and breath means life. This truth is also confirmed by Peter: "For prophecy never had its origin in the human will, but prophets, though human, spoke from God, as they were carried along by the Holy Spirit" (2 Peter 1:21).

We see then, not only did the Holy Spirit write the Bible, but He did so through the pens of men. Knowing the Holy Spirit, therefore, is not really optional for the Christian. It is vitally critical. Since we find the most thorough information about Him in the Bible, that will be our textbook. Because of that and even though I belong to a certain church denomination, I will not be writing as a denominationalist. My goal rather is to write as a biblicist. That means that everything I've been taught, everything others have said, every experience claiming to have its origin in the Holy Spirit, must have scripture as the final judge. Scripture (written by the Holy Spirit) will judge the veracity, authenticity, and integrity of all things said about and all experiences claimed to be from the Holy Spirit.

There is a term I learned in my early college days in psychology. It is *tabularasa*, which means a blank tablet. A clean slate—the mind before impressions are recorded upon it by experience. As much as possible, this has been my goal in writing this book. I want to know the Holy Spirit…don't you? But I don't want to be encumbered with, nor burdened by the insistencies of others. No. I want Him to write on my mind the truth about Himself. I hope you will join me in this same spirit.

May I ask you to do one thing? Would you ask the Lord right now to be your teacher? Would you ask Him to write truth on your heart about the Holy Spirit? He longs and promises to do this (John 16:13). It is a prayer He will surely answer in the affirmative.

There's one more thing I want to say before you start reading. Books about the Holy Spirit cannot be numbered. They are rather innumerable. So many are excellent and well written. The authors have written from their viewpoint (hopefully from what the Holy Spirit has taught them). For that reason, I have not tried to reinvent the wheel. I have not tried to say what others have said so well and frankly better than I could have said it. Nor have I written in a strict academic fashion. I haven't used the word *pneumatology* (numa-tol-ogy) anywhere. Pneumatology is the theological word describing the doctrine of the Holy Spirit (now you know). My book is just that: my book. It is, for the main part, autobiographical. Remember the title? *The World's Most Well-Known Stranger.*

The title suggests a deficiency in relationship. Not an academic deficiency necessarily. One may know accurate theological information about the Holy Spirit and yet never know Him. So the book is autobiographical. It is relational. It strives to be biblical to the best of my ability. The Holy Spirit's personage must not be sacrificed in pursuit of His power. Some do this.

I will maintain on every page the indispensability of the Holy Spirit in knowing Jesus Christ. This is the goal. This is the sweetness. We are made for Him and to know Him increasingly. The Holy Spirit sees that we do. By the time you get to chapter twenty-two, I hope that will happen to you.

Dan Robinson
Highlands, 2017

CHAPTER 1

DO I HAVE TO?

My heart pounds within me. I cannot keep silent. (Jeremiah 4:19)

S omeone once said, "Don't write unless you simply can't help it." Almost every writer understands that. There is a compelling…a mustness on the inside. Predictably this is how I feel about this book. I've been writing it for most of my life. Pieces of the truth have fit together from one source or another. The picture is becoming clearer. It is that picture that I'll be trying to describe throughout. It is the picture I believe the Bible presents about the Holy Spirit. I will enumerate this picture with five specifics. These are as follows:

1: WE CANNOT BE SAVED APART FROM THE HOLY SPIRIT

It is His responsibility to convict regarding sin, righteousness, and judgement (John 16:7-11). Among other things, this means that whenever the Christian evangelizes, there is someone we can't see who is also evangelizing. He is working from within the believer and upon the unbeliever. He truly is the Greatest Evangelist. This should encourage us. Many believers seem fearful and hesitant to share the good news of Jesus Christ. This is just one more reason why they shouldn't be.

2: EVERYTHING WE KNOW ABOUT JESUS IS BECAUSE OF THE HOLY SPIRIT (JOHN 14:26)

We can know about Jesus intellectually. We can even grasp theology academically, but a personal and intimate relationship with Jesus Christ depends on the faithful Holy Spirit teaching us about Him.

3: THE HOLY SPIRIT ALWAYS SHOWCASES JESUS (JOHN 16:14)

Church history has at times recorded some unusual events and phenomena. These manifestations have been attributed to the Holy Spirit. This is still true today. Yet the right question to always ask regarding all such claims is, *Where is Jesus in this? Does this demonstration before my eyes and ears draw my attention to the Son of God?* These questions are honest and necessary. Error regarding the Holy Spirit can result in error regarding Jesus. This, of course, satisfies our enemy's intent and can set us on a wrong course that might last a lifetime.

Furthermore, an experience of, with, or by the Holy Spirit seems, for some, to become an end in itself. Unfortunately, this has often been the case. That is much like setting out on a mile run and stopping before the mile is reached. We must not stop before glory, honor, and praise are unquestionably and clearly focused on Jesus Christ.

When we stop with experience only, we tend to glorify the experience. We reason, "I have had an experience and therefore it must be true, valid, and from God." We are then judging Truth (the Bible) by experience rather than judging experience by truth.

This is critical. The devil can and will give experiences. Discontented because he cannot create, he is left only with the option to imitate. My experience may be nothing more than overzealous flesh, or worse still, deception. When this happens, observers walk away very mindful of me and very unmindful of Him. It is a subtle trap.

Like John the Baptist, I must be wonderfully content to decrease while He increases. When I do, I am in harmony with the Holy Spirit. In fact, I will even be somewhat reticent about sharing my experience, as was Paul (2 Corinthians 12:1-16). This is so because I'm aware of the human heart's bent to simply have an experience! Such an experience may then be heralded, sought, and even emulated. When that happens, my experience of/with the Lord Jesus trumps the Lord of the experience. And it is the experience, not Jesus, that gets the glory. The Christian must be keen to this and ever aware of it.

4: THE HOLY SPIRIT IS THE TEACHER

Not only does He teach us about Jesus, He is in fact the resident Theologian. We've all had the experience of reading a book and thinking, *I am not quite sure what the writer is saying here. I wish I could talk to him.* This is precisely what happens when we consult the Holy Spirit, the Author of scripture.

This does not eliminate research, word studies, historical context, wrestling with the text...and more. All attended by an attitude of dependence demonstrated by prayer. We have to show up for class to learn from this Teacher just as we have to with any other teacher. Of course, He isn't any other teacher. He's the One who knows everything about everything, and when that "Aha!" moment comes to the Bible student, it is because of the Holy Spirit. When the text *jells* or *clicks* or *makes sense*, we know for sure the teacher is teaching.

My final reason is really the heart and soul of this book...

5: IT IS MY CONVICTION THAT THE HOLY SPIRIT IS INDEED THE WORLD'S MOST WELL-KNOWN STRANGER

Christians certainly know about Him. Any competent book on world religions would contain this basic doctrine of the Christian faith. The trifold benediction of, "in the name of the Father, Son, and Holy Spirit" has been heard for countless ages by countless numbers of people, and yet, for all of this (and more), the Holy Spirit remains a virtual stranger to many.

Those who do acknowledge Him seem to fall into two broad categories. One is the extremist. This person seems to gravitate to the bizarre, unconventional, and experiential. For this person, the more the better. It is not really about Jesus; it is rather about pursuing unexplainable strangeness. This is very dangerous. Like Simon the Sorcerer in Acts 8:9-23, their heart is not right. The Holy Spirit doesn't delight in strangeness. He delights in the Truth…both written and living.

The other category of persons could be described many ways. They are ecclesiastically polite and theologically orthodox. They are biblically informed. They've heard about the Holy Spirit all their Christian lives. They are good church-goers, but there is about them that which is conspicuous by its absence. There seems to be no life! I'm not suggesting they are not born-again (only God knows that); rather they seem to be a parade of religionists at their best. Even squeaky clean, yet no life. One may spend minutes or days with them, and in all of that time, there is no clear evidence of another Life indwelling.

What can we make of this? Maybe they have not been taught adequately. Maybe they feel self-sufficient. Maybe they are confused into thinking that church life and divine life are the same. But I really think many have just decided to play it safe.

On the one hand, the extremists have scared them, and on the other hand, they are going to heaven anyway…so why even bother with an intimate relationship with the Holy Spirit? Still for others, that which is most frightening is losing control. If the Holy Spirit is in control, then they aren't. Stated quite frankly, there are those in the family of God who prefer to lead rather than follow the Holy Spirit. The Holy Spirit will let them do that, and in so doing, it is their life, not the life of Jesus, that is seen. This is tragic.

These, then, are my reasons for writing this book, and I hope they resonate with you. There is never any reason for the Christian to be afraid of God or of what He does. The Holy Spirit is vital to every aspect of the Christian life. He is a careful and compassionate teacher. He will always take us to Jesus. He will always glorify Jesus. He will always reveal Jesus.

I hope you will accompany me on my journey in this book. I hope you will grow. I hope the biblical truth regarding the Holy Spirit will make you hungry…not afraid, and if He is only a well-known stranger to you, I hope He will become a well-known confidant and friend.

CHAPTER 2

TRACES OF LOVE

Come My Beloved...Let Us Go. (Song of Solomon 7:11)

C an any good thing come out of Nazareth?" was Nathaniel's question (John 1:46). He was simply echoing an incredulity that was the norm of his day. We might say it like this: "Surely a prophet of God wouldn't come from little-no-name-obscure Nazareth," all the while forgetting that God does as He pleases in heaven and on earth.

To my point: who would have ever thought that God would use a member of a well-known rock band of the late '60s to introduce me to the Holy Spirit! The music of the Classics IV can still be heard today on oldies-but-goodies radio stations. Their recordings include, "Everyday with you Girl," "Spooky," and "Traces of Love"—to name a few. The organist was named David Phillips.

I first met David around 1969. We were both living in Ocala, Florida. He drove a Ford Mustang and helped himself gingerly to the cold beer sufficiently cooled in an ice chest in the trunk. He invited me, by the way, to borrow his car any time I wanted. I did, even though I had no driver's license at the time. David wore shoulder length red hair, a zip-up striped jump suit, and black leather boots. At every point, he looked and carried himself as a perfect reflection of the late '60s culture in America, and he was far away from the Lord. His mother was Ruby Phillips. My parents, Bob and Mary Robinson, worked with her in the Bible, Book, and Music Store in Ocala. All were praying for David. It so happened that my dad, like David, was also an accomplished keyboardist. It was this love for music that drew us all together and drew David to our home.

The year 1969 eventuated into 1973. During college spring break, I hitchhiked from Tampa, Florida, to Asheville, North Carolina. On the way, I stopped and stayed over near Jacksonville with David and his wife. In the course of four years, he had changed indeed. The outside looked different. The inside sounded different. His mother's prayers, and others, had been answered. Having left the Classics IV, David was then playing the organ at his church.

The next morning, David took me to my I-95 drop point. As we said goodbye, he gave me a little book about the Holy Spirit. I tucked it away and stuck out my thumb. Several hours later I arrived home. The book had been read, and I was hungry; as you might guess, the hunger was not for food.

The Holy Spirit about whom I was reading was drawing me… inexorably so. By that time I had already been a Christian for ten years. I had been called to preach for three years. Yet I was still carnal. There wasn't much to distinguish me from a lost, unsaved person. I didn't know it then but do now: I was missing what I already had! The Holy Spirit was present in me, He just wasn't preeminent. I don't know frankly if I'd ever given Him a thought.

At the time, my Grandfather Miller owned a farm with some fifty acres. Near the back side of the property there was a little cabin. My Uncle had constructed that cabin perhaps twenty years earlier. My grandfather gave it to me. It afforded me wonderful solitude. It is torn down now, and I still miss it. That little 14 x 20 one-room cabin became a sacred place. Driven by what I'd read in the book, I found myself on my knees in my cabin. Then and there the Lord revealed Himself to me. How He did that is not the issue. That He did is the issue, and He will do the same for you or anyone who seeks Him. I had turned the corner, and I knew it. I experienced an immediate turning of my heart toward the Lord. This wasn't emotionalism. This was obedience.

The Holy Spirit already living in me took me straight to the greatest commandment found in Matthew 22:37-38. Jesus said,

"Love the Lord your God with all your heart and with all your soul and with all your mind. This is the first and greatest commandment." Frankly, I was overcome. Just as the law of aerodynamics overcomes the lesser law of gravity (hence, airplanes fly), so likewise the greatest commandment to love overcame all the lesser things I had given my life to—and not a few of those things religious and churchy. The Holy Spirit was working in me. Theretofore I had not known such clear and definable work. I was only nineteen then. Many decades have since passed. I have sought to know the Holy Spirit in increasing intimacy. This quest always resulted in a deepening relationship with the Lord Jesus Christ. In case that sounds to you like bragging, I want you to know that I know every turning of my life, and yours, toward Him is only because He has first turned to us. So if any man boasts, let him boast in the Lord Jesus Christ.

Ahead of me, from then until now, lay school, school, and more school…marriage, children, pastoring, international missions, writing, teaching, multiple heartaches and joys, including the death of my first wife. However, the Holy Spirit now had His right place in my life. That meant that Jesus had the right place, and what began as only traces of His love in 1973 have deepened into strong, bold lines. His grace has brought me safe thus far and is continuing to lead me toward home, but, oh how much I needed to learn. How much I needed grounding. Just a few years later that process began in earnest.

CHAPTER 3

WHO IS THE
HOLY SPIRIT?

To meet God is not to get answers to our questions; it is to learn the right questions.
(Ron Dunn)

A t this point, would you stop and ask yourself that question? (The title of this chapter.) I do not remember ever having asked the question, but certainly the answer began during my second semester at seminary.

My professor of evangelism began lecturing on the Holy Spirit. Now nearly four decades later, I still have those notes. By now I have fleshed out his insights into my own simple outline.

1. *The Holy Spirit is a person to be given acceptance.* So many refer to Him as an "it." That is an insult to Him even as it would be to you! Such a reference to Him may indicate a lack of knowledge, intimacy, or even indifference. I really do not believe, however, that anyone would deliberately insult the Holy Spirit.

   It may simply be their sincere but scrambling attempt to say something about someone about whom they know so little! Yet the Lord Jesus graciously taught us in John 16:13-14, "But when He, the Spirit of Truth comes, He will guide you into all the truth. He will not speak on His own; He will speak only what He hears and will tell you what is yet to come. He will glorify me." I count seven pronouns all referencing a person. Since He is a person, then it follows that He can be...

    a.   Resisted (Acts 7:51)

    b.   Grieved (Ephesians 4:30)

    c.   Outraged (Hebrews 10:26-30)

    d.   Blasphemed (Matthew 12:31)

    e.   Tested (Acts 5:9)

    f.   Fellowshipped with (2 Corinthians 13:14)

    g.   Communicated with (John 14:26; Romans 8:16)[1]

As a person, He naturally has all these attributes of personality. As a person, He can be known, but first I must settle this issue of personhood. I cannot know an "it." I cannot become acquainted with an experience. This Person of the Holy Spirit is living inside every believer (1 Corinthians 6:19). In so doing, He has done everything necessary to afford you the possibility of an intimate relationship with the living God through His Son, Jesus Christ.

The table is set. There is a place for you. Come and eat. Discontinue imaginations about the Holy Spirit. Discontinue trying to make Him in your own image and to your expectations. The Holy Spirit is a person. Get to know Him. You have a whole lifetime in which to do it.

2.   *The Holy Spirit is also a presence to be acknowledged.* We've all been ignored at times. Overlooked. Treated as if we didn't exist. What a terrible affront that is! The same treatment can be rendered to the Holy Spirit. Jesus told us plainly that the Holy Spirit is with us (John 14:17), and because of that incredibly clear statement, it is no less than remarkable how the Christian can live, seemingly without any sense of

---

1.   In a pamphlet booklet, *Studies of the Holy Spirit* (page 8), prepared by Dr. Jack Gray and distributed to his students at Southwestern Baptist Theological Seminary in missions class in 1977.

His presence! Perhaps the most outstanding evidence of this is in our praying. We frequently hear or say in prayer, "Lord Jesus, be with us." There's no question regarding the sincerity of that prayer, but we must question the necessity. *Why would I ask for something I already have?* It is not His presence for which I should ask, but rather awareness of His presence, which I already have!

How much we need to learn at this point, and it does take a lifetime. With this, we must remember that while He is neither touchy or petulant, He nonetheless can be grieved. When he is grieved, He withdraws not His presence, but rather His power. This is at least one explanation for powerless Christians. I see this often in worship services. It is both from the pulpit and in the pew.

For example, a well-meaning preacher may step to the platform and begin his remarks with a joke. Certainly there is nothing wrong with godly humor. Jesus had a marvelous sense of it. But, in the preacher's well-meant intentions to connect with the congregation, he's disconnected with the Holy Spirit! The Holy Spirit may well have had another direction for that worship hour. Indeed the singing, praying, leading up to the sermon time have all suggested a certain attitude aim of the Holy Spirit, but the preacher has missed it. It is a grievous thing to watch that happen. A man must simply be sensitive to the Holy Spirit. Sometimes the Holy Spirit does lead with light-hearted godly humor. Not so at other times. The man who has been called to rightly handle the Word of Truth is responsible to ascertain that direction and follow it.

On the other hand, this sort of thing can generate from the pew. Men and women may be busy chatting, joking, or a hundred other things. This sort of non-preparation, pre-occupation makes it very difficult to hear, sense, and worship the Lord. It is convicting to remember that whatever spirit I allow in me as I come to worship is the spirit that influences worship.

A deeper question then is, *Am I ready to meet Jesus?* This is what worship is about. I am coming into His presence. In so doing, surely I would prepare myself at least as much as I would, should I be coming into the presence of any earthly dignitary. The level of casualness and serendipity that seems to characterize much of the church here in the West should be a very deep concern for all of us. The Holy Spirit is indeed a presence. He honors the bride of Christ by being present. It is proper therefore and fitting that we acknowledge His gracious presence.

3.   Finally, *the Holy Spirit is a power to be appropriated.* This is indeed thrilling! This is not the puny earthly power of mere men. No. This is the very omnipotence of God now indwelling every believer. This is really remarkable and cause enough for celebration. This was the very promise of Jesus in Acts 1:8: "But you will receive power when the Holy Spirit comes on you, and you will be my witnesses in Jerusalem, and in all Judea and Samaria and to the ends of the earth." Yet it is painfully obvious that many in the body of Christ either don't know this truth or do know it and fail to appropriate it. Is the power of the Holy Spirit operative in your life right now? I certainly hope so. This is His promise and your privilege.

The pressing question then is, how is this power appropriated? The answer is, power is determined by what authority I'm under. Think about this for a moment. Why does a policeman have power? He has power because he is under the authority of the state. He has no power in himself, yet he represents incredible power. He therefore is responsible to simply carry out the authority placed in him by those over him.

We see this principle illustrated clearly in scripture. In Luke 7 we read of the centurion. His servant was about to die, so the centurion sent inquirers to Jesus to ask for help. Yet even while Jesus was in route to the centurion's house, He received this word from the centurion's friends:

"Lord, don't trouble yourself, for I do not deserve to have you come under my roof. That is why I did not even consider myself worthy to come to you. For I myself am a man under authority with soldiers under me. I tell this one 'Go' and he goes; and that one 'Come' and he comes. I say to my servant, 'Do this' and he does it" (Luke 7:6). It is as if the centurion is saying, "Lord, I understand fully how this authority issue works. I am a man under authority, and because of that, I represent and become a channel for the very power of Rome. Likewise I see that you are a man under authority, and therefore you represent and become a channel for the very power of God."

We say again: power is determined by what authority I'm under. A person under the authority of Jesus Christ has the power of the Holy Spirit. A carnal Christian cannot claim this. A carnal Christian is under their own authority. Therefore, they are under their own power. Most of us have been there, haven't we? We've discovered there is not really any power at all—only frustration. Yet we may appropriate the promised power of the Holy Spirit. To do so we must come under the authority of Jesus Christ. Then…please don't overlook our Lord's resounding response! He said, "I have not found such great faith even in Israel." By our Lord's own definition, great faith is not doing this miracle or that impossibility. It is coming under authority! When we do that, He declares that our faith is great! It is by that faith that we appropriate the power of the Holy Spirit. Please don't settle for less. Some do. They prefer a program over His Person. A performance over His presence. A predictability over His power. These are simply stuck in the rut of churchianity. Don't get stuck. Remember who you are and whose you are. On the Cross, Jesus gave His life for us. In resurrection, He gives His life to us. It is in the Person of the Holy Spirit.

CHAPTER 4

THOSE PASSAGES IN ACTS

False ideas are the greatest obstacles to the reception of the Gospel.
(J. Gresham Machen)

M any Bibles have the editorial superscription, "The Acts of the Apostles," when identifying the book of Acts. More accurately, however, we should name it, "The Acts of the Holy Spirit." While only a handful of the apostles are mentioned—Peter, James, John, and Paul (and mightily so)—the Holy Spirit is seen and "acting" in every situation and on every page.

In four of these situations we find truth that is critical to our understanding of the doctrine of the Holy Spirit. These four passages are Acts 2:1-11, 8:1-25, 10:9-48, and 19:1-6. Admittedly, these passages are the fodder for misunderstanding, misinterpretation, and hence misapplication. Yet I believe we'll find, in our study, those passages to be as clear as day. So before we give our attention to each of those scriptures, I want to suggest some guidelines we'll follow.

THE BOOK OF ACTS IS TRANSITIONAL

Transitional is not transitory. The Word of the Lord (Acts) endures forever (1 Peter 1:25). Neither is transitional optional. It is the very bread by which we must live (Matthew 4:4; John 6:35). Transitional rather is just that. Acts is going from one place to another place. It is a moving book. It is a video versus a still. Illustrations of this are multiple.

We see the church birthed in Jerusalem and then spreading to the uttermost parts of the earth. A transition. Peter is front and center as leader in Acts 1-12. That leadership role then shifts to Paul in chapters 13-28. Another transition. There is also critical transition in the gospel audience as well; first the Jews...then the Gentiles. Again, while the church in Jerusalem retains her "mother-church status," the church in Antioch assumes a major role in missionary outreach. These are all significant transitions in the Books of Acts. It is a transitional book.

WE MAY FURTHERMORE REGARD ACTS AS PROGRESSIVE REVELATION

By progressive revelation I mean that one revelation builds on another. Progressive revelation is complementary and supplementary. It is not contradictory. Progressive revelation is just that: it is progressive. It is transitioning from one revelation to the next. Each one perfectly timed by a holy God as He reveals more and more of Himself in succeeding biblical revelations. We see this dynamic clearly reflected in God's revelation of the Holy Spirit.

In the Old Testament, the doctrine of the Holy Spirit was general...almost to the point of obscurity. To be sure, the Holy Spirit is clearly present in creation and upon the prophets as well as in many other ways. However the brush-strokes of His work, while critically indispensable, are deliberately broad. The doctrine of the Holy Spirit unfolded in the Old Testament is wonderfully anticipatory of the New Testament. I hope you don't hear me under-valuing the Holy Spirit's presence in the Old Testament. At the same time I hope you do hear and see the perfection and purpose of our God in this process. At this point it may be well, therefore, to establish a principle from which our study will unfold. It speaks to God's perfection and purpose.

Regarding the Father, Son, and Holy Spirit Trinity, it may be said: The Trinitarian example establishes equality in value while maintaining distinctives in function. The Father, Son, and Holy Spirit are co-equal. One is not more valuable than the other, yet clearly their functions are different. We see God primarily in the Old Testament, the Son in the Gospels, and the Holy Spirit in the church age. Each one a Person of the Trinity. Each one fulfilling a distinctive function. The Holy Spirit's function unfolds distinctively in the book of Acts. Again we see this anticipatory and progressive dynamic even in our Lord's own ministry. The most thorough doctrine of the Holy Spirit comes from His own lips. We find this teaching in John 14–16, but this doctrine doesn't unfold until we get to Acts. Therefore, regarding Acts in its transitional nature is key to its proper interpretation.

EXEGESIS VERSUS *EISEGESIS*

Do you know these terms? While somewhat technical, they are, nevertheless, quite simple in meaning. They are pronounced "x-a-ge-sis" (*exegesis*) and "ice-a-ge-sis" (*eisegesis*). In each case, the prefix is a preposition in the Greek New Testament, hence "ex" meaning out of and "eis" meaning into. Whether we know it or not, we employ these methods of Bible study each time we come to the scripture. We either "get out" what is there, or we can bring to or *into* our scripture study something that isn't necessarily there. Do you see the problem? Frankly, the Bible will preach itself. It is inexhaustible in truth. The job of the Bible student is to get out what's there. But it is work!

A seminary level of training, however, is not required. The Bible aides that are available to us are endless. Furthermore, biblical truth is not finally a matter of intellect. The Holy Spirit is our teacher. It is He who must pronounce His nod of approval on all our Bible study. We must hear Him say, "This is what I mean by what I wrote." Anyone who is teachable may know this sort of teaching. So in regard to our present study, I think we do see the problem. Many read into (eisegesis) the scripture their own ideas about the Holy Spirit. These ideas can originate from anywhere to everywhere, and they may or may not have biblical foundation. When this happens, we judge or draw conclusions about scripture based on what we've merely heard or experienced (as I mentioned in chapter one)—yet it is scripture, not my experience or my own ideas, which must be the final judge.

Reading into scripture my ideas about the Holy Spirit can lead to all kinds of conclusions. Many of which, I'm sorry to say, have no biblical basis for a foundation. But when I come with an attitude of prayerful exegesis, I find the Holy Spirit a willing and capable teacher. Not only will He guard me from error but He will do so by unfolding the Truth I am reading or studying.

I hope to encourage you at this point. Why not be like young Solomon who confessed his absolute dependence on the Lord (1 Kings 3:7)? He asked God to give him a discerning heart. God did that, and He will do it for you also. The Holy Spirit is a clear and patient teacher. He desires that we know the truth about Him. This is imperative because knowing the truth about Him is to know the truth about Jesus. So let's keep in mind as we study the Holy Spirit in Acts, not "What my experience says it shall say," but in fact what it does say!

TESTIMONY AND TEACHING

I was first introduced to this idea by James McConkey in his book titled, *The Threefold Secret of the Holy Spirit*. He says, "We have confined ourselves too closely to the apostolic experience instead of the apostolic teaching at Pentecost."[2] This does indeed seem to be the case and I believe accounts for no small amount of confusion.

In application, then, we may say that the testimony of any two Christians is necessarily different. But the truth by which they are saved must necessarily be the same. One deals with experience, which is personal and individual. The other deals with the means of salvation, which is biblical, unchanging, and universal. There is only one way to get saved. It is through faith in Jesus Christ, repentance from sin, and confession of Him as Lord and Savior. That's the teaching part. It is absolute and unequivocal. However, the way that

---

2.   James McConkey, *The Threefold Secret of the Holy Spirit*. (Pittsburg: Silver Publishing Society, 1897), 12.

truth is received (when, where, how) will differ with every Christian. That's the testimony part. I now can draw some conclusions about the Holy Spirit.

It is imperative that I know biblical doctrine (teaching). It is not imperative that I have the same experience (testimony). A quiet, meditative Christian may be just as full of the Holy Spirit as a demonstrative, extroverted Christian. Holy Spirit fullness is not an issue of style but of substance. Trying to make your experience mine is like trying to wear your clothes: it is foolish, ill-fitting, and defeating for one Christian to insist on the same experience of another. It is wise, prudent, stabilizing, and healing, however, for every Christian to insist on the truth of biblical doctrine. All of us will have changing testimonies, however, based on changeless truth. If we will take care of the intent (our motive), He will take care of the extent (the manifestation).

PRAYER

The Bible is a book of history, poetry, and prophecy. One may well be able to grasp the facts of the Bible while still missing its meaning. Its meaning requires revelation. This is given by the Holy Spirit when we pray. This is so because in addition to being a book of history, poetry, and prophecy, it is a spiritual book. It is the very mind of God on paper. It is written by Him through the pens of human authors. We are so bold as to say the meaning of scripture indeed cannot be ascertained apart from prayer. When we pray, we are asking the author to tell what He meant by what He wrote.

Understanding the Bible is more than gathering facts. It is primarily the means whereby we may know the Father more intimately through the Son. It is the Holy Spirit who facilitates this goal. The book of Acts, then, is incredibly significant at this point. It is the launch pad of the church. It is the springboard of the era of grace. It is the initiation of worldwide evangelism. It is the pacesetter until He returns.

The doctrine of the Holy Spirit infused in this book is to be regarded therefore with carefulness and teachability. We must hear what it says (exegesis) and not try to make it say what it does not (eisegesis). This is accomplished as we study and pray. I hope you will do just that. In fact, I hope you will maintain an attitude of prayer throughout.

The Holy Spirit is the teacher. Ask Him to show you where, if anywhere, you've brought eisegesis into your study. Ask Him to help you be willing to let go of cherished ideas and pet theologies. This is hard for most of us. Ask Him to make you a student of the Word. Become a Word Christian. Let the Word of Jesus Christ dwell richly within you (Colossians 3:16). As Spurgeon said, "Let your blood be Bibline."[3] In all of this, resist being a Bible-beater. Be a person of grace. Live the truth as much, or more, than you quote it. Be winsome and attractive in your spirit.

Remember, the Holy Spirit is presenting Jesus through you. This is His job and ministry. He loves to—insists upon—showcasing Jesus, and He will do that through you. Acts, after all, is the continuation of all that Jesus had only begun to do and teach (Acts 1:1). He now continues His ministry by fulfilling what He and His Father had promised: the baptism with the Holy Spirit (Acts 1:5; John 14:16-18, 26; 16:12-15).

---

3.   Charles Spurgeon, "The Last Words of Christ on the Cross," in *Spurgeon's Sermons*, vol. 45, #2644, (Spokane, Washington: Olive Tree Bible, 2010).

CHAPTER 5

THE CLEAR PURPOSE OF TONGUES IN ACTS 2

My gracious Master and my God, assist me to proclaim to spread through all the earth abroad the honor of thy name. (Charles Wesley)

S ome regard Acts 2 as the Holy Spirit's debut. Others cite it as a proof-text for speaking in tongues. Still others hold this great chapter as the model or platform for the present-day church. They say, "What we need is another Pentecost." What then *is* Acts 2 about?

Certainly the Holy Spirit assumes a preeminence not heretofore seen in scripture. But it is not His debut. The phenomenon of tongues is frankly thrilling to read about. But there is no hint that this be the experience for all Christians for all times in all places.

If finally, someone means the present-day church needs a great outpouring of the Holy Spirit, then count me in; but to insist on replicating uniformity of that time, culture, and history is, I believe, limiting the Holy Spirit. He is moving the bride of Christ ever forward to her wedding day. Pentecost was foundational in that procession, however the "more" of the Holy Spirit is before—not behind—us.

It is my conviction, therefore, that the epicenter of Acts 2 is evangelism, not tongues. This is in perfect accord with the great heart of God. He, the Holy Spirit, is *always* going after a lost human race. He is always drawing people to faith in Jesus Christ. On the day of Pentecost, some three thousand were thus dealt with. In this pursuit, *tongues were the method, not the message.*

This goal of evangelism seems implicit in Luke's mind. He mentions almost casually in Acts 2:1, "When the Day Pentecost came." This is where we should start in our understanding of Acts 2. Luke is establishing the context for us. We naturally ask then, *What is Pentecost? And what is its connection with the rest of the story?*

Pentecost was an annual event—observance. It was one of three festivals in which the presence of all Hebrew males was required (Deuteronomy 16:16). The other two were the Feasts of Unleavened Bread and Tabernacles. Pentecost marked the beginning of the summer wheat harvest. Harvest time is about an ingathering. It is the time to reap what has been sown.

The Lord Jesus Christ had been mightily sowing seeds of truth throughout His earthly ministry. His crucifixion, resurrection, and ascension now having been completed, it was time for the ingathering-harvest. This harvest was His. It belonged to him. He was the First Fruit (1 Corinthians 15:20).

This centrality of evangelism was indeed promised by the Lord. He said that the disciples witness for Him would begin in Jerusalem (Acts 1:8). The gracious accompaniment of tongues wonderfully facilitated this witness, and what an extraordinary facilitation it was! Luke uses such words as "bewilderment" (vs. 6), "utterly amazed" (vs. 7), "amazed," and "perplexed" (vs. 12). Translated, these words mean, "to confound or perplex" (vs. 6), "to put out of its place, to be beside oneself with wonder, admiration and reverence" (vs. 7), and "to be utterly at a loss" (vs. 12). Such superlatives are deliberate. This was indeed unprecedented! No Day of Pentecost like this one had ever happened before. What so amazed the audience that day was hearing their own ethnic dialect. We might call it their native tongue. It would be like you or I traveling to some remote region on earth and being greeted in English. The ears of the listeners were hearing the wonders of God in their own tongues (vs. 11). No interpretation was necessary!

So again we remind ourselves that the Holy Spirit always points to Jesus. This is precisely what happened in Peter's subsequent sermon (Acts 2:14-40). Are you aware, then, of the identifying and distinguishing characteristics of these tongues when compared here to the tongues in 1 Corinthians 12 and 14? We do so at this point because there is frequently a blurring of these two events, even an insistence that these passages teach the same things. Some years ago, I received the following chart. I believe it helps us see clearly the differences in these two events:

Acts 2	1 Corinthians 12 & 14
Known Tongues	Unknown Tongues
No Interpretation Necessary	Interpretation Necessary
Purpose: Evangelization of the Sinner	Purpose: Edification of the Saint
Demonstrated at the Birth of the Church	Demonstrated in the Established Church
A Tongue-Shaped Flame	No Tongue-Shaped Flames
Tongues Associated with Filling with the Holy Spirit	Tongues Associated as a Gift of the Spirit
The Promise by the Father	A Gift of the Spirit
The Purpose Is Power	The Purpose Is Praise

Perhaps there are other distinctives you might find. However, there are some very clear conclusions.

1. The *only* unequivocal constant in both accounts is the Person of the Holy Spirit.

2. The purposes of the Holy Spirit are painstakingly obvious in their differences.

3. The responsibility of every Christian is to evangelize. Indeed, it is a command. It is not the responsibility of every Christian to speak in tongues, nor are we ever commanded to do so.

4. The convicting truth is that my tongue, known or unknown, is influenced by the indwelling Spirit.

In summary, then, we are maintaining that the purpose of tongues in Acts 2 is evangelism. Tongues were the method. Jesus is the message. The Holy Spirit was responsible for both.

It is instructive to us then (again) that the Holy Spirit always glorifies Jesus. He is the one who introduces us to Jesus. He never oversteps this priority by giving any other priority to anything or anyone else. Under the Holy Spirit's tutelage, all roads lead to Jesus. If we live under this radically clear doctrine, we also will be trusting the Holy Spirit to enable us to speak convincingly about Jesus. Predictably, then, we see this pattern also in our remaining three passages: Acts 8:1-25; 10:9-48; 19:1-6.

CHAPTER 6

SAMARIA

As soon as we discover a new insight into our Faith, we are transported with joy like a miser who has found a treasure. (Francois Fenelon)

S ometimes the Holy Spirit teaches by repetition. This is why we find some truths of the Bible repeated over and over again. The themes of salvation, grace, and the love of God are among these repetitions. On the other hand, sometimes the Holy Spirit teaches one thing, one time. It is not repeated. It is solitary. For example, the Red Sea divided one time, and the prison doors opened for Peter supernaturally one time. Likewise, then, these solitary themes/events should catch our attention as much as the repeated ones.

The way the Holy Spirit worked in Acts 8 was unique. It was solitary. It was not repeated. What happened in Acts 8 had never happened before. Furthermore, it was never mentioned again. It stands alone. This is very important to our study because there are some who seem to miss these very dynamics and then go on to build a theology on it.

In Acts 8 we see the one-time event where men and women receive the Holy Spirit *after* their conversion (vv. 15-17). It is this very event that has fostered the current idea that the Holy Spirit is received sometime after salvation. We might call it a two-stage conversion. This erroneous idea suggests there is something more for the Christian than Jesus; it is even called the second blessing! However, there is nothing more than

Jesus! It is He whom we receive in salvation...never subsequent to it. The Person of the Holy Spirit will always take us deeper in Him. He will never take us beyond Him. It isn't possible to go beyond Jesus. In Him dwells the fullness of the Godhead bodily, and in Him we are complete (Colossians 2:9-10). Complete means complete!

With that said, however, we do still have to grapple with Acts 8. We do so by beginning with what we know for sure. For example, we know for sure that the men and women in Samaria were really saved. This is clear in verse twelve. The word *believed* is a verb denoting a completed action. They didn't need to believe anything else. Philip's preaching of the good news was evangelistic. The Samaritans heard how to be saved and, in fact, were. There is no basis to suggest they weren't really saved or that they needed to believe more in order to be saved.

The second truth we know for sure is that the Holy Spirit is continuing His pattern of evangelism. In Acts 2, the Holy Spirit drew Jews into the church. He did this through the unprecedented methodology of tongues. In Acts 8, He is drawing Samaritans into the church, and He did this, also, through another unprecedented methodology, namely, receiving the Holy Spirit after salvation.

We must again note His consistency of evangelism. We have seen the Holy Spirit do this before, and we will see Him do it again. This doesn't change. This should greatly encourage us in our own personal witness and evangelism. The Holy Spirit is going after unsaved people, and He does that through saved people. We see this precisely in Acts 8.

Furthermore, we also know for sure that Samaria was part of the geographical region prophesied by our Lord in Act 1:8. He said the evangelism of Samaria would take place. In Acts 8 it is exactly that which is happening. So, frankly, those details and others all add up to and agree with a biblical, changeless model for salvation, all except for the post salvation receiving of the Holy Spirit.

I suggest three reasons for this anomaly. The first is for the sake of the Samaritans. The enmity and hostility between the Jews and Samaritans was intense. It is very difficult to cite any modern-day equivalent. Their repugnance for one another had its beginning in the Old Testament.

The year was 722 BC. The Assyrians invaded and took captive the vast majority of Israel. At that time, Israel was the common-collective name for ten of the twelve tribes. Following King Solomon's reign, the original twelve tribes were torn by their own civil war. Two tribes (Judah and Simeon) settled in geographical Southern Israel.

Their capital was Jerusalem. They called themselves Judah. They were also known as the Southern Kingdom.

As mentioned, the remaining ten tribes settled in the northern geographical region of Israel. This capital was Samaria. They called themselves Israel, and they were also known as the Northern Kingdom. Each kingdom had twenty kings, respectively. While usually fighting against one another, they would at times form an alliance and fight together against a common enemy. The Southern Kingdom lasted until 586 BC, when they were overthrown and deported by the Babylonians.

But back to the Assyrians and 722 BC. Those Jews not deported, but left behind, intermarried with the Samaritans. The result was a mixed race. Over time, significant and seemingly irreparable tensions multiplied among the Jews and Samaritans and Jewish Samaritans. This eventuated in the Samaritans establishing a worship center at Mt. Gerizim in Samaria. The Jews continued worshipping at the temple in Jerusalem. Furthermore, the Samaritans held only to the first five books of the Old Testament—the Pentateuch. They, unlike the Jews, did not embrace the entire Old Testament as authoritative. By New Testament times, the tensions between Jews and Samaritans were deeply entrenched. These were racial, historical, doctrinal, and as a result, personal. Of course, I hope you've already been thinking about Jesus and the Samaritan woman in John 4. Again, this is an anomaly. It is a departure from the norm, He, a man…she, a woman. He, a Jew… she, a Samaritan. He, a worshiper in Jerusalem…she, at Mt. Gerizim. He defies social customs and racial tensions. His goal was to introduce her to the spring of living water. She accepted His offer and, because of her testimony, many of the Samaritans believed (John 4:1-24).

For all of these reasons, it was imperative that the Samaritans be included in salvation, unquestionably and conclusively so. Again, for these same reasons, they seemed the most unlikely to be saved. The air of enmity was thick and unyielding. The salvation, therefore, of the Samaritans was no less than stunning! Nonetheless, an undeniable fact. Remember? Acts is progressing. In this progression the Holy Spirit is going after all races, cultures, and nations. What had heretofore been an exclusivity (Jews do not associate with Samaritans, John 4:9) was now becoming an undeniable inclusivity. This was—most simply put— gargantuan. There could be absolutely no mistake. God orchestrated the unusual details of Acts 8 for this very purpose! So very unprecedented was the event that God called attention to it by orchestrating it! The Jewish Messiah was also Savior to the Samaritans!

A second reason for this irregularity points to a fundamental truth of scripture. God is no respecter of persons. In this instance we may say that He gives the gift of the Spirit to any and all Christians. There is an uncomfortable one-upmanship attitude among some Christians at this point. It speaks of spiritual elitism. Some gifts are regarded by some Christians as absolutely essential. Non-negotiable. The possession of these certain gifts—or a gift—marks one Christian as more spiritual than another one. This position is a terrible and gross affront to the Holy Spirit who gives gifts as He pleases and draws whomsoever He will to Jesus. It is all by the grace and pleasure of God. This message was loud and clear to the church at Jerusalem. It may, frankly, have also been a shock, but the irrefutable evidence was in. This evidence leads us then to our third reason for the irregularity.

Peter and John were dispatched by the Jerusalem church for the very purpose of investigating and confirming the salvation of the Samaritans. It was well understood that their conclusions would be impeccable. They were, after all, the church pillars. But remember, this is Peter and John, and did they ever have their own prejudices!

Remember, first of all, that John, along with his brother James, had wanted to call fire down from heaven to consume the Samaritans! (Luke 9:51-55). John had a huge bias against the Samaritans. God sends him to the Samaritans! Furthermore, and much later on, John writes about the presence of every tribe, language, people, and nation being in heaven (Revelation 5:9; 7:9). He is also called the apostle of love. John got it, didn't he? The gospel is for everyone. The Samaritans were his primer course for this truth.

Then what about Peter? Luke moves us rather quickly to Acts 10. There, Peter discovers the gospel of grace is not only for the Samaritans, but also for the Gentiles. It was not only necessary but kind of the Holy Spirit to lead Peter one step at a time into this great truth. Acts 8 was the beginning step. For the most part, our brother Peter was an extremist. He was either all or none. The salvation that Jesus offers is for the whole world. Once Peter got this, he was all in.

In conclusion then, Acts 8 was a divine aberration. We have tried to underscore the reasons why. Understanding these reasons surely deepens our love for the Holy Spirit's methods and tenacity. He is crossing every imaginable barrier to draw people to Jesus. He did it then and is still doing it today.

CHAPTER 7

SURPRISE, PETER!

What does my Lord Jesus Christ order me to do? (Francis of Assisi)

Acts 10 begins the fulfillment of Acts 1:8. The ends of the earth include everyone else—from then until now—as the audience to be reached with the gospel. If we're not careful, however, we'll read this tenth chapter as a sudden turning of God to the exclusively non-Jew: the Gentile. Furthermore, we are apt to read it as a precedent. A new thing. A sort of final outreach to those yet unreached. Yet with only a few minutes of reflection, we remember that not only was it *not* a new plan to reach the Gentiles, it was indeed always *the* plan.

The word *Gentile* means ethnos. We immediately recognize our English *ethnic* as a derivative. It can mean pagan, heathen, nation, or even people. In biblical terminology, *Gentile* would reference a non-Israeli—a non-Jew. Yet it was this very people that God promised to bless through Abraham! God would make Abraham a great nation, and through him, all the families (tribes, race, people) on the earth would be blessed (Genesis 12:1-3). The evangelism of the Gentiles in Acts 10 began in Genesis 12! Furthermore, Paul reminds his readers that the Gentiles were once "Separate from Christ, excluded from citizenship in Israel and foreigners to the covenants of promise, without hope and without God in the world. But now in Christ Jesus, you who once were far away, have been brought near by the blood of Christ" (Ephesians 2:12-13). While Abraham, then, was the initial recipient of the promise, there were others in the Old Testament who specifically applied it.

Two outstanding Old Testament personalities help us at this point. One, Elijah, had no trouble ministering to the Gentiles. The other, Jonah, never got over his trouble! Let's take Elijah first. In the days of Israel's unblushing and bold idolatry, God sent an unblushing and bold prophet. We remember him best for that incredible showdown on Mt. Carmel (1 Kings 18). Elijah was not one to be trifled with. He was seemingly without peer, and his departure from earth was just as remarkable as was his ministry on earth. He went to heaven without dying (2 Kings 2)!

But's there's more. Just prior to Mt. Carmel, Elijah made a visit to Zarephath (1 Kings 17). There he was sustained by a poor widow. Although convinced of her own imminent death due to starvation, she fed the prophet. Then she did it again. And again. The fact is, she and her son never ran out of food! God honored her faith. She did not die, but her son did! Elijah then cried to the Lord on behalf of the boy, and life returned to him! This is the first instance of raising the dead recorded in scripture. Adding to this already remarkable account, we discover two more things: (1) Zarephath was the headquarters for Baalism, the false religion of godless Jezebel, and (2) the widow was a Gentile! She became a believer in the God of Israel. We see again that reaching the Gentiles was not a new plan. It was always *the* plan.

Yet not all prophets are alike. While the story of 1 Kings 17 might be obscure to some, certainly the story of Jonah is well known by many. Again, I submit the big story here is not the big fish. The story is how Nineveh, a Gentile city, populated by tens of thousands, repented at Jonah's preaching and were spared God's judgment. Jonah didn't like this, couldn't understand it, and was angry with God because of it (Jonah 4:4).

In these stories, we begin to see the tip of the iceberg. If there was hostility between the Jews and Samaritans, then it was exponentially so with the Gentiles. Generally considered as pagans, the Jews were loath to admit them into the grace of God.

All of these reasons explain Peter's sincere declaration, "I have never eaten anything impure or unclean" (Acts 10:4). Respectively, these words mean profane, common, and desecrated (impure), and lewd, foul, or unthinkable (unclean). God responds by declaring, "He has made clean that which Peter has insisted is unclean" (Acts 10:15). It is the same word used by Matthew, describing the cleansing of the lepers (Matthew 8:1-3).

Ultimately, Peter declares in Acts 10:34-35, "I now realize [i.e., to grasp or perceive with the mind] that God does not show favoritism [i.e., an acceptor of faces]." The idea is that while we may be awed or unimpressed with this or that person when we see their faces, God isn't (Acts 10:35), but He accepts from every nation (i.e., ethnos, meaning multitudes, or those nations distinct from Israel or Gentiles) the one who fears Him and does what is right.

Peter, being the gifted preacher that he was, then, launches into his sermon (Acts 10:34-43), and again, as in Matthew 17, God interrupts Peter: "while he was still speaking...the Holy Spirit came on all who heard the message" (Acts 10:44). The tense of the verb suggests that which is, at one and the same time, both initial and final. It signifies completion. This is Luke's way of telling us that the Gentile listeners who were "hearing the message" (Acts 10:44) were soundly convicted by the Holy Spirit and converted. The salvation transaction was completed!

Again, notice the unchanged pattern in our study. It is the Lord Jesus Christ going after the entire world in the Person of the Holy Spirit. That day, He used Peter. In our day, He will use us. Peter's compatriots were astonished at this (same as Acts 2:7, 12), but not Peter! Peter's astonishment was settled on the rooftop only a few days earlier. They were astonished that the events they were witnessing were so very similar to the events of Pentecost. These Gentiles were speaking in tongues, and when compared to the wording of Acts 2:11, we believe these tongues also were probably known—not unknown.

Peter simply declares, "They have received the Holy Spirit just as we have" (Acts 10:47). What a statement! Not a hint of Jewish exclusivism. Peter's job was to simply present the truth. The Holy Spirit's job was to convict and draw men to faith in Jesus Christ.

He has followed the same pattern since Acts 2. Methods, times, and culture change—the message doesn't. This same pattern is ours as it cannot be improved upon. We present Jesus Christ. We do so clearly and with grace. We have no authority to insist on a certain experience or emotion. If we will simply do our part, the Holy Spirit will do His, and His part is to bring whosoever will into a personal relationship with Jesus Christ.

CHAPTER 8

ACTS 19: CLOSING THE LOOP

I Did It My Way. (Jaques Revaux, Gilles Thibault, Paul Anka)

W hen I read Acts 19:1-7, I immediately think of many post-war stories. Before the Internet and its instant communication and news, there was a time when news traveled slowly or even not at all. For this reason, there are accounts of soldiers fighting on even after a war is officially over. Such was the case with the Civil War in America, WWII in the Pacific, and our brothers in Acts 19. Hence their words in verse 4: "We have not even heard that there is a Holy Spirit." What began as "sincere though crude and ignorant"[4] concluded with them receiving the Holy Spirit and speaking in tongues (Acts 19:6).

Our first question, then, is not what happened between verses 4-6, but rather what happened before. Starting in Acts 19:1, our attention is drawn to Apollos. We know from Acts 18:24 that he was quite a gifted orator. His credentials all seem to be in place except for one pivotal caveat: "he knew only the baptism of John" (Acts 18:25).

---

4.   Archibald Thomas Robertson, *Word Pictures in the New Testament*, vol. 3 (Nashville: Broadman Press, 1930), 311.

This immediately qualified him to have the ways of God explained to him more adequately "by our brother and sister, Aquila and Priscilla" (Acts 18:26). And it was this same baptism, only of John, which these twelve men at Ephesus had received (Acts 19:3-7).

John's baptism was a pre-Pentecostal water baptism. It was (Paul explains in Acts 19:4) a "baptism of repentance." He said, furthermore, that those hearing John were to believe in the one coming *after* him— that is, in Jesus. Apparently these twelve men were in somewhat of a news vacuum. John had been dead for some twenty-five years by then, and while these men believed (Acts 19:2), likely they, like Apollos, needed more explanation. Some scholars, therefore, identify them as "Old Testament Saints" only. Furthermore, their level of belief is not clear. Surely they were walking in the light they had received. They simply had not received all the light as it is in Jesus.

Paul seems to be immediately keen to this anomaly. Hence his question: "Did you receive the Holy Spirit when you believed?" (Acts 19:2). In other words, something was askew in Paul's mind. He is immediately alerted to something in his spirit. He asks the question precisely because it *was* the norm to receive the Holy Spirit upon believing! Again, those men were sincere, but their understanding only partial.

The one whom John promised would baptize with fire and the Holy Spirit had indeed come (Matthew 3:11). Yet further demonstration of the Holy Spirit and fire came at Pentecost. These twelve were wandering in a theological fog somewhere in between. However, upon hearing the truth about Jesus from Paul, they were then baptized in Jesus' name—no longer just in John's name. Now, indeed, they were Christians. New Testament Saints—no longer just Old Testament.

The demonstration of tongues, at this point, was a gracious act of the Holy Spirit. These men needed tangible evidence. They, furthermore, needed clear theology. Ephesus was, after all, a critical location for the gospel (Acts 19:8-41), and in this we see the pattern we have been observing all along; the Holy Spirit is all about the preaching of Jesus to the end that all people everywhere may hear.

At this point in Acts, that worldwide effort is complete in the initial stages. The church has now gathered Jews, Gentiles, Samaritans, and Old Testament Saints into the body. In each case, the apostles were there to verify that all had received the Holy Spirit. Indeed, biblically they had all been baptized in the Holy Spirit—signaling conversion of life, not a demonstration of a gift. God's purpose was clearly inclusivity, not exclusivity.

This is a good word for us today. You already know that the mention, or even teaching, about the Holy Spirit can be divisive. How sad and tragic! He is inclusive. He ingathers, and what He absolutely insists upon for every believer is glory to Jesus Christ. He insists—unequivocally—on *nothing else!* The Christian—and then the church who embraces this truth—will, because of its unity, attract the power of the Holy Spirit and will expedite the evangelizing of all peoples. This will be to His glory and the fulfillment of His promise to be His witnesses to the ends of the earth.

CHAPTER 9

SELAH

Even in the busiest life, there is a place where we may dwell alone with God in eternal stillness. (Streams in the Desert)

I feel rather certain you recognize the word *Selah*, found predominately in the Psalms. It means silence, pause, or rest. That is what I want us to do here. Let us reflect on what we have said and draw some conclusions, and then we will resume our study.

THE HOLY SPIRIT IS A PERSON

Jesus used personal pronouns to describe Him: "The Holy Spirit *whom*" (John 14:26), "I will send Him" (John 16:7), and "When He comes" (John 16:8). Since He is a person, then I must continue getting acquainted with Him. He is not an aberration, nor is He a disembodied will-o'-the-wisp. I cannot know an aberration or a mist.

THE HOLY SPIRIT POINTS ALL ATTENTION TO JESUS

"He will glorify me" (John 16:14). His primary function is not to give me an experience. Though He may well do that, it is not primary. If He does do that, then I must not insist that my experience become someone else's. Nor is He an emotionalist. He does not come to give me a certain emotion. He never does His deepest work (glorifying Jesus) in our most shallow part (our emotions). But again, there will at times be the sweet and satisfying emotions as in any other intimate relationship, only on a different level—a higher plane.

I could say much more at this point, but it does seem that when/where there is a misunderstanding about the Holy Spirit, it comes precisely at this point. Some regard Him only as a giver of an emotional experience. This is as far as they ever go. Yet this is only the tip of the iceberg…and indeed may not even be that much!

THE WORK OF THE HOLY SPIRIT IN ACTS WAS ONE OF INCLUSIVITY

Jesus, in the Person of the Holy Spirit, indwelling every believer, was fulfilling His own command to go into all the world to make disciples. Bringing people to Jesus! Unbelievably, this "New Testament epicenter truth" is missing from much conventional preaching/teaching about the Holy Spirit. This truly is difficult to understand. When the Holy Spirit is "given the floor," He will talk about Jesus. When believers are given the floor, they will often talk about an experience or a gift. There is a disconnect here that every serious believer will seek to overcome.

THE HOLY SPIRIT IS *ALWAYS* COMMITTED TO THE HIGHEST GOOD

Although not explicitly mentioned, but I hope clearly implied, the Holy Spirit is *always* committed to the highest good in the believer. This never changes, and the highest good is a molding of the believer more and more into the likeness of Jesus (Romans 8:29). This takes place at the absolute discretion of the Holy Spirit, and it is inclusive of the "all things" of Romans 8:28, and, simply enough, "all things" indeed means just that.

The crushing heartaches, spiritual mountain tops, any/all gifts of the Holy Spirit, sickness, unanswered questions, criticisms, accusations, promotions, demotions, straight As, straight Fs,

54

answered prayers, unanswered prayers, unfair treatment, hope, and hopelessness…and more and more and more and all and all and all!

God the Holy Spirit is working "all" things together in the believer's life so that he or she will increasingly and convincingly show Jesus. This is why we must continue knowing Him. This increasing relationship enables us to facilitate rather than frustrate His purpose.

I hope this encourages you! It is not even possible for you to face *anything* that is beyond the helping, comforting, strengthening ministry of the Holy Spirit. He will treat you as Jesus would if Jesus were still walking in a physical body on the earth. He will bring you to Jesus. He will reveal Jesus to you.

So rest in these truths, won't you? Pause in these truths. Consider the incomparable love of Jesus Christ for you, and in awe and silence, contemplate His infinite closeness to you right now. *Selah*.

CHAPTER 10

THE ONLY PLACE

The Christian who is filled with the Holy Spirit can be compared to a glove. Until it is filled by a hand, a glove is powerless and useless. It is designed to do work, but it can do no work by itself. It works only as the hand controls and uses it.
(John MacArthur)

U p to this point, I have tried to address what has seemed to me to be misinterpretations about the Holy Spirit. My comments have been based primarily on the book of Acts. I now want to move to the book of Ephesians. My reference is to Ephesians 5:18-21. This is an absolutely marvelous passage regarding the Holy Spirit. It is, furthermore, crystal clear in what it sets forth:

> *Do not get drunk on wine, which leads to debauchery. Instead, be filled with the Spirit, speaking to one another with psalms, hymns, and songs from the Spirit. Sing and make music from your heart to the Lord, always giving thanks to God the Father for everything, in the name of our Lord Jesus Christ.*

The reason I've titled this chapter, "The Only Place," is because this passage in Ephesians *is* the only place in all of the Bible wherein we are commanded to be filled with the Holy Spirit. I hope you will read that sentence again. Frankly, it is somewhat startling in its utter simplicity and clarity. It necessarily, by its own authority, lays to rest other spurious and unsubstantial arguments set forth regarding the baptism of the Holy Spirit. By way of introduction, therefore, I want to talk about the baptism in, and fullness of, the Holy Spirit.

I make the distinction in these terms only because scripture does. One may be baptized in the Holy Spirit and yet not be filled with the Holy Spirit. On the other hand, everyone who is filled with the Holy Spirit must necessarily have first been baptized in the Holy Spirit. Confused? It seems that many are. Yet, there is no confusion in the Bible. Only clarity.

Let us take first the term *baptism*. It means, quite simply, to immerse or place under. Jesus used it in reference to the afflictions and the ill-treatment He was to receive (Luke 12:50). He said He had to undergo this "baptism." For Him, the Cross meant being placed under—immersed in—agony and rejection beyond description.

Of course, water baptism is much more familiar to us. When one is born again, one is baptized in water. This is the correct order. Water baptism is the outward sign of an inward commitment. Biblically it always follows salvation. It never provides it. Only Jesus saves. One who is baptized only is not a Christian, but a Christian will certainly want to be baptized.

So we must take this fundamental meaning of being immersed in or placed under and apply it to the Holy Spirit. We find it in 1 Corinthians 12:13. In the NIV it reads, "For we were all baptized by one spirit so as to form one body, so it is with Jesus Christ." When studying the original text, we discover the word *baptized* is plural. Therefore, it is true of every Christian. It is also past tense. Now we conclude that baptism of the Spirit is not something yet to be done for the believer. It is indeed proof that one *is* a believer.

Contrary to popular usage of the phrase *baptism of the Holy Spirit*, referring to something extra or more or indicating a certain spiritual gift, none of that is mentioned here. Rather, it is clear that baptism with or by the Holy Spirit is both simultaneous and synonymous with conversion. When a person becomes a Christian, he or she is baptized in the Holy Spirit.

Again, popular usage of the phrase frequently forms itself in a question. It would sound like this: *Have you received the baptism of the*

Holy Spirit? The one asking almost certainly means, *Have you had an experience subsequent to salvation, evidenced by speaking in tongues?*

The Christian may very well have received the gift of tongues (or one of many other gifts). Those dynamics are not in question here. What we are questioning on a biblical basis is the misunderstanding—even the error of—the Christian expecting something he or she already has! We reiterate: every Christian is baptized in, with, and by the Holy Spirit. If this hasn't happened to someone, then that someone simply isn't a Christian. Gifts and fullness of the Spirit are separate issues from baptism in, with, and by the Holy Spirit. One must be born again by the Holy Spirit before one can receive gifts and fullness of the Spirit.

Additionally, as I have already mentioned, this biblical misunderstanding and misinterpretation fosters a certain pride in the body of Christ. It is the "haves" against the "have nots." It is one-upmanship. It is the "really spiritual" versus the "also-rans" (unsuccessful competitors). This is terrible. It is the competitive spirit of the disciples all over again, isn't it?

After Jesus spoke to them for the second time regarding His death, all they could think about was who was going to be the greatest (among them) in the kingdom (Mark 9:30-37). Mark it well: humility—not bragging—most fully identifies those who are full of the Holy Spirit. Whatever our Father may give us, and everything our Father does give us, is to be received with a humble attitude.

Finally, something happens in the misunderstanding/ misinterpretation of baptism of the Holy Spirit, and this is the most egregious. Stated quite simply and sadly, *Jesus is eclipsed!* I have known very few devotees of this erroneous doctrine of Spirit baptism who emphasized Jesus more than the Holy Spirit. To the contrary—it is the Holy Spirit and the gifts that take center stage.

The Bible never endorses this position. Anything that eclipses Jesus is, by default, considered greater than Jesus. But no one or no thing is greater than Jesus, and any emphasis otherwise ought to set our hearts trembling. In distinction, therefore, from baptism in the Holy Spirit, we find in the New Testament there are multiple accounts of multiple *fillings* with the Holy Spirit. We see initial filling in Acts 2:4. We emphasize initial, for there are many more listed. For some, however, their entire theology regarding the Holy Spirit starts and stops right here. How sad indeed when this happens. Not even to mention how much is lost.

The scripture goes on, nevertheless, to record many fillings of the Holy Spirit…both individually and corporately. Notice these: (1) Acts 4:8—Peter; (2) Acts 4:31—all believers; (3) Acts 9:17—Saul-Paul; and (4) Acts 13:9—Paul again. These are the *recorded* instances. It is indicative of a normal pattern. A Christian may expect multiple, even innumerable fillings with and by the Holy Spirit. These instances in Acts were initial, not final. Courage, holiness, being equipped for ministry, and confronting evil were all occasions for fillings with the Holy Spirit.

This is one of Luke's favorite words. He uses it in Luke 1:15, describing John the Baptist, who "will be filled with the Holy Spirit even before he is born." He also uses it negatively to describe the people's reaction to Jesus. Found in Luke 4:28, "all the people in the synagogue were filled with thumos"—wrath towards Jesus. So much so, they intended to kill him by throwing Him off the cliff.

In every instance recorded by Luke in both Acts and his Gospel, the word *filled* means to be filled or to be full, wholly imbued, affected, or influenced with or by something.[5]

Critical to our study, and conspicuous by its absence, is *any* reference in *any* of these passages to tongues or baptism (Paul's baptism in Acts 9:17 refers to water). This should fill us with great encouragement. Baptism in the Spirit is an initial and non-repeatable event. It is when I receive the Holy Spirit at conversion. Fillings are multiple, repeatable, and technically limitless.

In coming to Ephesians 5:18-21, we find those distinctions sharply focused. This is where we find the clear unfolding of the doctrine of the fullness of the Holy Spirit. There is, however, a challenge here for us. Namely, will we read the text in light of what is says (exegesis) or read into it what we want it to say (eisegesis)?

This requires something from us. I must be teachable. I must listen to the teacher. This will almost certainly mean letting go. This is painful. It is so painful that some simply will not do it. They will associate this text with a certain person, time, or experience and what

---

5.   Spiros Zodhiates, ed., *The Complete Word Study Dictionary: New Testament* (Chattanooga: AMG Publishers, 1992), 1175.

it meant to them then. It is even possible that those dynamics claim one's allegiance more than truth. So why don't you pray just now:

> *Lord Jesus, I want to know the truth about your Holy Spirit and fullness. I thank you for your faithful Sovereignty over my life. You've wasted nothing. I submit to you my teaching and my training, which have brought me now to this point. Where there's been truth, I ask you to confirm it. If there's been error, I ask you to correct it. Teach me, Lord Jesus, what it means to be full of the Holy Spirit. I ask in your name. Amen.*

Now, trusting and expecting our Lord to do just that, notice the following about Ephesians 5:18-21.

THE COMMAND TO BE FILLED WITH THE HOLY SPIRIT

This is the idea in the original wording (Ephesians 5:18-21). It is imperative or a command. Furthermore, it is plural. Did you know that all Christians everywhere are under orders to be filled with the Holy Spirit? There is nothing exclusive about that! It is the incumbent responsibility on all. We note additionally this command is in the active voice. This means continuously or all the time.

We note finally that this verb is passive. That means that something must be done for me, but that takes place only when I meet certain conditions, whereby that command may be realized in my life.

In translation, we may read Ephesians 5:18 like this: "All of you Christians—yes, every Christian—stay continually, 24/7, full of the Holy Spirit." As already mentioned, then, most Christians are very surprised to discover that this is *the only time* in the entirety of scripture where we are commanded to be filled with the Holy Spirit! Conversely, we are nowhere commanded to be baptized in the Holy Spirit. Why? Because that baptism—for the Christian—has already taken place. It is simultaneous with conversion (1 Corinthians 12:13). When we become Christians, we are placed into Christ (i.e., we are baptized into Him). "In Christ" is one of Paul's favorite and most repeated phrases. This is what may be called positional truth. Since it is a position, it is changeless. The Christian is in Christ. Christ Jesus is in the Christian. That will never change.

It is helpful and encouraging to say it this way: He accepts us based on His own and unchanging indwelling presence within us, not on our changing performance. I hope you will rest in that. It seems many Christians are frantically trying to get from Him what is already theirs in Him. Acceptance. This is positional truth.

Because of this position—baptism in Christ Jesus—we can draw several conclusions:

1. Every believer is indwelt by the Holy Spirit. This indwelling occurs at conversion. It identifies us as sons and daughters of God (Romans 8:14-17).

2. Every believer is baptized by the Holy Spirit (1 Corinthians 12:13).

3. Every believer has all the Holy Spirit there is. This comes as a surprise to many. Fullness is not when I get more of Him; it is when He gets all of me! Did you ever hear the story of the two little sisters who were competing against one another for their own sense of preeminence with their father? Tauntingly, one of them climbed into her daddy's lap and said to her sister, "I have all of daddy there is!" Shyly the other sister also took her place on the daddy's lap and pressed just as closely as possible. To her sister, she said, "You may have all of daddy there is, but daddy has all of me." This is fullness!

   Think of it theologically for a moment; if fullness were getting more and more of Him, then it would follow that at each preceding step, I would necessarily have less of Him. Since *He is* salvation, then it follows that if I don't have all of Him, then neither do I have all of salvation. Continuing this line of reasoning, I could end up *partially saved*, which can only mean *fully lost!* Everything salvational hinges on the fact that we indeed receive all of Him at conversion.

4. While every believer is indwelt by the Holy Spirit, every believer is not infilled with the Holy Spirit. Indwelling is His presence within us wherein we respond to what he has done on the Cross. This response is repentance, confession, and faith.

Fullness, on the other hand, is His unbridled presence through us wherein He responds to what we have done. What we do is obey. We deliberately bring our lives and plans under His authority. This is the changing of masters. This is the smiling approval of Jesus over the entirety of my life. Fullness lives out the truth: "It is no longer I, but Christ who lives in me." Fullness doesn't require our experience; it requires obedience.

So now we've said four things about this command to be filled with the Holy Spirit. Let's summarize:

1. In every believer He is resident but not president. Present but not pre-eminent.

2. Indwelling is initial, non-repeatable, and cannot be lost. Infilling is repeatable, ongoing, and *can* be lost (not salvation, but fullness).

3. Fullness is not the demonstration of any certain gift but the domination of my personality. The idea of *being filled* in Ephesians 5:18 clearly means total control. The New Testament suggests a person may be controlled by faith (Acts 6:5), or anger (Luke 6:11), or even fear (Luke 5:26), and in our text, be controlled by the Holy Spirit.[6] Are you?

THE CONSPICUOUS FRUIT OF THE HOLY SPIRIT

Moving now to Ephesians 5:19, there is what I call the conspicuous fruit of the Holy Spirit. This really is the heart of the matter. This is so because this is the only place in the New Testament where the *evidence of fullness follows the command!* This is not fruit as Paul discusses it in Galatians 5. That is a result of abiding. But here is the immediate, obvious, verifiable evidence found in one who is Spirit filled. Our text suggests this fruit is four-fold.

---

6. John MacArthur, *The MacArthur New Testament Commentary: Ephesians* (The Moody Bible Institute of Chicago, 1986), 250.

SPEECH

"[Speak] to one another with psalms, hymns, and songs from the Spirit." We see then the first evidence of Spirit fullness is not that I speak in tongues (as some teach), but rather that the one tongue I have be controlled. The sense of the word suggests a willingness to engage. Jesus in you is willing and interested in engaging others. Furthermore, the "psalms, hymns, and songs from the Spirit" indicate the flavor and attitude of my words.

My words carry a certain atmosphere about them. I'm not interested in the latest lingo or cultural phraseology. (By the way, the current "in" words as I now write are *back in the day, awesome,* and *perfect*). Some Christians argue that one should use these words in order to identify with our culture. A need, by the way, Jesus never expressed or had. Rather than our words being *cool,* they are to always be with grace, seasoned, as it were, by salt, so that we will know how we should respond to every person (Colossians 4:6). I hope you understand this. This truth isn't chaining us to always talk church talk or feel compelled to say something religious. Rather, tone and wholesomeness typify the words of a Spirit-filled believer. Reportedly, it was Spurgeon who said, "Holy talk following upon meditation has a consoling power in it for ourselves as well as for those who listen." I think this is huge, don't you? Have you come to the point where you are touch sensitive to the Holy Spirit restraining your words? It is as if He is saying, "Not this; not here; not now."

The flip side is equally true. This is where He releases you to speak. It is a word spoken in due season. It might be a word of exhortation, rebuke, healing, encouragement, or joy. But it is the word of the Spirit through you! This is normal for every Spirit-filled believer. It then follows naturally at this point to remind ourselves that we're never more full of the Spirit than we are of the Word. Spirit–filled Christians are men and women of the Word. Their hunger and thirst is always, *What does God say?* The Holy Spirit always takes us to the Word He Himself has written. This is truth! It is strong. It is everlasting. It is authoritative. It is this environment of the Word that seasons the expression of my words. A Spirit-filled Christian is identifiable by what they say and how they say it. The very first evidence the truth cites of being full of the Holy Spirit is one's speaking, both content and manner. Incredible, don't you think? Following the text, then, we come to the second evidence.

SINGING

Do you have a song in your heart? I'm not speaking of being coaxed or cajoled into singing. Rather this singing comes from the indwelling resident singer. We already know that He is rejoicing over us with singing (Zephaniah 3:17). It must then naturally follow that He is also singing within us. There is within the Spirit-filled person's heart, a melody.

At times it seems that we become only slowly aware of this singing. Like a knocking at the door at night time, our consciousness dully awakens to the sound. Our dullness may be due to preoccupation or non-expectation (the Holy Spirit singing?) or simply a lack of biblical education. Nonetheless, as the Spirit is the speaker and thus influences our speech, so, likewise, He is the singer and thus influences our singing. The word Paul uses for singing is *ado*. This word is always translated, "Praise to God" (Colossians 3:16; Revelation 5:9; and 14:3).

Now it would seem (dare we say it?) that while anyone may sing hymns (lost people and carnal Christians as well), it is only the Spirit-filled Christians whose singing is considered praise in heaven. Why is this so? It is so because praise necessarily decentralizes self. Praise is *other-ness*. That other-ness is God Himself! Indeed, the Son Himself! The Holy Spirit delights in orchestrating praise to Father and Son. True worship is being consumed with Him, not with me. Praise can take place in the seemingly most anti-praise places. Praise is not giddiness. It is not coercion by some high-powered song leader. Praise rather acknowledges His Presence. The Holy Spirit awakens and alerts me to my Father's peaceful and powerful Presence, no matter what.

A Christian can go through the most tragic times, experience obstacles never thought possible, and endure long tedious days and longer tedious nights. However, with that Christian is the very presence of Holy God, overseeing, superintending, directing, sustaining. Praise is transforming on the inside. Praise teaches us to live on God alone (as John Bunyan learned in his Bedford imprisonment). Sometimes the Spirit-filled Christian will praise the Lord inaudibly, within their own hearts. At other times the praise may be verbal. Praise can be very demonstrative or hardly noticeable at all. This is the sweet mercy of the indwelling, infilling Holy Spirit. I may praise with all my heart as the praise leader directs my heart.

Before we leave this subject of praise, I want to suggest three principles regarding its validity.

1. *My authenticity in corporate praise* (a setting of many Christians in a church or conference, etc.) *is inseparably linked to my personal private life of praise and worship.* It is entirely scriptural to conclude that my praise be continual. I, therefore, come to public worship meetings not to get pumped up but to continue with other believers what I've already been doing. My sense of integrity, however, warns me of the possibility of hypocrisy. I have been forbidden at times by the Holy Spirit to sing certain hymns.

    Does this sound strange to you? "My Jesus I love thee, I know thou are mine. For thee all the follies of sin I resign." At times that hasn't been true in my own heart. In those times the Holy Spirit has graciously convicted me, warned me of hypocrisy, and drawn me to confession so that indeed I might resume the song before the singing is over!

    My public worship must be authentic before the Father. Ideally it is a continuation of what I've already been doing in private.

    Alternately, consider this dynamic from a completely different angle. It is entirely possible for me to come to church absolutely under it. The strain and worries of my life have taken their toll. I am dead to the things of God. The last thing I want to do is sing; but remember, praise welcomes His presence. Because of this corporate praise, Jesus draws near. By sheer will power, I open my mouth and sing. This is not hypocrisy. This is obedience. God always honors obedience. His presence cheers me. His majestic shepherd's heart ministers to the very depths of my being. He has honored my two little fishes and five loaves of bread and multiplied it! He honors praise, He inhabits praise, and He directs praise. The Holy Spirit indwelling-infilling the Christian will bring a melody of praise to Father, Son, and Holy Spirit.

2. A second dynamic of praise (when we are singing) is that *the words of the music must be accompanied by the melody…not overcome by it.* This truth is not original with me, but it is so incredibly insightful. Sometimes a melody of a song can overcome the content. When this happens, I am more soulish than spiritual. Another way of stating this truth is that the words of a hymn or praise chorus should be able to stand alone or on their own. The words should direct my thinking to the one I'm worshipping—not the rhythm or pleasant sounds. If the words alone don't move me, then it is probable that the melody alone will, and when this happens, I can be mightily stirred in a worship service but unfortunately left utterly unchanged in life.

    Martin Luther said, "next to theology I give my first and highest honor to music."[7] This puts worship and praise in the proper sequence.

3. Thirdly, *it is one's life—not talent or musical ability—which becomes the highway of praise to God.* Man and message, life and lip, public and private. These dynamics must coalesce into seamless symmetry. It is unanimity among these factors that authenticates one's praise. We must always look for the life behind the music. This is so in my private worship. It is true as I follow a public worship leader.

    I think what I'm trying to say is there's no need to ever be overly impressed with yourself or with others. I don't want you to be disappointed when a public worship leader is found out to be less than what you expected. This is particularly true in our day of instant, comprehensive, and international communication and media.

---

7. Martin Luther's Table Talks #7034.

Someone (almost at once, it seems) can become a star overnight in the Christian world. He or she is the latest "Johnny-come-lately." Then sometimes, some of them disappoint. Cynical? No, and I am thankful for that. It is just that I've lived for more than six decades now, and I know that what happens after the cameras stop running is more important than what happens as the cameras are running. Talent, musical ability, and the latest and greatest will come and go, but the Word of the Lord endures forever!

SENSE OF SOVEREIGNTY

A sense of sovereignty is the third evidence of the Spirit. In Ephesians 5:20 we read, "always giving thanks to God the Father for everything, in the name of the Lord Jesus Christ."

The Bible clearly, and without apology, assumes the existence of a sovereign God. It, furthermore, gives one confirming verse after another. We read in Romans 11:36, "For from Him and through Him and for Him are *all* things." Does that leave anything out? The psalmist says it like this: "You have assigned me my portion and my cup" (Psalm 16:5). The original language suggests to enumerate, weigh out, and appoint. I dare say that because of this truth, there can be no real accidents in the Christians life—only appointments.

An accident, by definition, is something unforeseen or not planned. There is nothing unforeseen or unplanned by our Father. If indeed He works all things together for good, then He must control all things. Our problem with sovereignty is our limited vocabulary and intellect. We find ourselves using words such as *permit, cause,* or *allow.* We follow up with the questions, *How could a loving God permit/cause/ allow...?* I hope you're not offended, but those questions are a bit like an ant trying to figure out a human being! It simply isn't possible.

The complexities and intricacies of a human brain are simply beyond an ant's ability to comprehend. Then again, we're not ants! We are, rather, made in the image of God. We are indwelt by His Holy Spirit. He promises wisdom and insight from His Word. Indeed, this is the very impartation of His own mind. All of this, however, is faith based. It is neither theory nor academia. It is absolute truth. What a huge difference it makes in everyday living. Delays, traffic jams, financial crisis, and everything else is supervised by our Father. This supervision is always for our good. This is the truth of Romans 8:28-29. Our challenge is to redefine *good*.

We typically consider *good* as the absence of bad or difficult things. The biblical definition, however, is, "looking—living more and more like Jesus." Read verse 29 again. Frankly, I don't know of anyone in scripture or Christian history who grew in Christlikeness apart from difficulty—even unfathomable extremities.

We read in Psalm 119:71, "It was good for me to be afflicted so that I might learn your decrees." How stabilizing it is to rest in the hands of the one who knows and controls all things! This is not que-sera-sera, what will be, will be. That philosophy assumes an invisible fate. No one is at the controls. Faith, on the other hand, sees someone at the controls and in perfect control. History is at every point His-story. He began it, He will conclude it—and somehow *every* event is purposeful in that progression. This is true internationally, historically, and personally.

What about Satan? (We are bound to ask). Isn't he behind calamity? Difficultly, etc.? Only as a secondhand instrument. This is the sustaining and unequivocal posture of scripture. He does roam the earth. He does command an army of demons. He is a formidable foe. Yet the Christian can say with Martin Luther, "We tremble not for him." Why? All of his activities are permitted and controlled by our Father.

There is not (as some Christians envision) a sort of holy tug-of-war going on between heaven and hell. God gains a bit, and then the enemy gains a bit, and so on. The only "rope" involved between heaven and hell is the rope our God allows the enemy to hold. It is specific and measured. Our Father has plans and designs. Satan *cannot* go beyond what the Father prescribes. Period.

Job is the outstanding Old Testament illustration of this. Peter is the great encourager in the New Testament. We read in Luke 22:31 how Satan demands permission to sift Peter. Did you see that? *Permission.* Jesus gave the permission. He had a plan for Peter's good in all of it, and, like Peter, the Christian can rest in the fact that every piece of ground we walk on has been prayed over by Jesus. Satan acts only by permission. I believe this permission can only come from Jesus *or* the believer. This is why we are taught in scripture to not give the devil any place. If it were not possible to do that, we would not be told to *not* do that. For some Christians, their troubles result from their own willful and sinful decisions. God's sovereignty never annuls man's responsibility. We do reap what we sow. Still again, our Father works all things together for our good. This involves (mercifully) even the worst decisions we've ever made.

A Spirit-filled Christian will give thanks in all things. He will do so in the name of Jesus Christ. That is to say, the Holy Spirit within the believer acknowledges the irrevocable truth that Jesus is indeed Lord over all things, all people, for all time. He is sovereign.

SUBMISSION

Finally, we come to the fourth fruit of being continually filled with the Holy Spirit. It is submission. Only a secure person submits. Neither the insecure nor the weak will submit. Jesus was secure and strong. He thus submitted to His parents (Luke 2:51), His Father (John 4:34; 8:29), and to evil men (John 19:11). He could do this because He was full of the Holy Spirit (John 1:14).

You may already know the basic meaning of submission is to arrange under. It has the idea of an orderly and pleasing arrangement. We could say that a stove in a living room or a lawn mower in a bedroom would be neither pleasing nor orderly. Both are out of place. A stove goes in the kitchen. That's where it fits and functions. A lawnmower works on the lawn. That's where it fits and functions.

A non-submissive Christian likewise cannot and will not fit or function properly. This is an immediate fruit of Spirit fullness. Not only is there a readiness to submit, but there is a peace to do so. I don't have to jockey for position, nor have the last word, nor play one-upmanship, nor make my opinion known on every conceivable topic! I am at rest coming under people, circumstances sovereignly ordered by my Father.

When a Christian submits to the speed limit, they are demonstrating faith (Romans 13:1). When a wife submits to her husband, she is demonstrating faith (Ephesians 5:22). When children submit to parents, they are demonstrating faith (Ephesians 6:1). Isn't this incredible to you?

There is so much non-biblical hype about Spirit fullness. Great *this*! Unusual *that*! Yet, submitting is indeed great! It is indeed unusual.

It is truly the work of the Holy Spirit. However, there are times when this work of the Holy Spirit will direct the Christian to not submit.

The principle is that when man's law contradicts God's law, then God's law must be chosen. We see this in Acts 5:29. The apostles, after having been forbidden to teach or preach in the name of Jesus, did precisely that! Peter's words were, "We must obey God rather than man" (Acts 5:29). This principle accounts for the underground church, the smuggling of Bibles and Christian literature into closed countries, and other illegal activities by Christians. They are obeying God rather than man. Some will pay for this with their very lives. They, more than anyone else, know and accept this. Jesus promised as much. Are you a Spirit-filled Christian? I hope so, because indeed every Christian is commanded to be such.

Can you see the substantiating fruit of fullness? Speech? Singing? Sense of sovereignty and Submission? Frankly, does not the control of one's tongue strike you as convincingly miraculous? (See James 3:1-12.)

All of this comes down to simple obedience. A Christian who loves Jesus Christ wants to obey Him. This is not slavish, legalistic bondage. It is trust and obedience, for there is *no* other way to be happy in Jesus. Are you still looking for—expecting—an "experience"? Why? Isn't Jesus enough? When we have Him, don't we have everything? *Do I still believe there's more than Him?* Although there's always more *in* Him, there's never more *than* Him.

THE CONSCIENTIOUS FILLING OF THE HOLY SPIRIT

Just like every other command of scripture, there does come a point in time when I obey. So if you're following my outline, I've talked about,

1. The Command to be Filled with the Holy Spirit,

2. The Conspicuous Fruit of the Holy Spirit, and now…

3. The Conscientious Filling of the Holy Spirit

This is now a deliberate decision every Christian must make. Often we pray, *Lord, fill me with the Holy Spirit.* I believe what we mean by that prayer is that we want all that He has, all that He is. It is another way of saying, "Fill me with you." It is a sincere prayer.

Yet, clearly, Spirit fullness hinges on our doing something to which He responds by doing something! Remember that we said "be filled" is a passive verb? That means He does something, indeed, only after we've met the conditions. Remember that fullness is not when we get more of Him, but rather when He finally gets all of us!

Obedience really is a simple process. I suggest you find a quiet, private place, open your heart to the Lord, and follow these basic guidelines as the Holy Spirit leads:

1. Ask the indwelling Holy Spirit to search your heart. Ask Him to point out any and all unconfessed sin. This process, although initial, is also perpetual. It is ongoing. Give the Holy Spirit time! He does a thorough job. Remember, there are many sins that we don't consider sin. Prayerlessness, judgmentalism, a critical spirit, and overeating—to name just a few.

2. Don't rationalize or justify at this point. Make no excuses. The Holy Spirit makes no mistakes. If He calls it sin, then you call it sin.

3. Agree with Him. Confession is to "say the same thing."

4. Then ask Him, *Are there any areas in my life not under your Lordship?* This question is comprehensive. It includes family, money, plans, ethics, purity, entertainment, literature, habits…on and on and on. He is Lord of all! To be full of His Holy Spirit is to be under His control.

5. One by one, yield these areas to Him. Acknowledge His absolute right to rule and reign over His own.

6. Thank Him for His perfect faithfulness and fullness. He delights to bless you and fill you as you let Him!

7. Fullness is nothing less than Jesus living in you. If this is what you want, then you will find heaven in full and happy agreement with you. Charles Inward has said, "There is no such thing as a once and for all fullness of the Spirit. It is a continuous supply from Jesus Christ Himself. A moment by moment faith in a moment by moment cleansing and a moment by moment filling. As I trust Him, he fills me. As

long as I trust Him, He goes on filling me. The moment I begin to believe, at that moment I begin to receive. As long as I go on believing, Praise the Lord, I go on receiving."[8]

8. Learn to live a dethroned life. If you have done all of the above, then you have just deposed yourself. You have abdicated the throne of your heart. This abdication becomes a moment-by-moment decision. Spirit fullness is Jesus Christ sitting on the throne of my heart.

The chief shepherd takes full responsibility for His sheep. And a smart sheep discontinues trying to satisfy himself from his own pastures and waters. A smart sheep gives up leading his own life and learns the sweet fellowship of following Him. However, this whole transfer of power and rulership is nothing less than traumatic. Spirit fullness doesn't happen apart from your willingness to die daily and your appropriation of death with Jesus Christ two thousand years ago. My willingness for Spirit fullness underscores my commitment to my own cross. It seems that so much teaching about Spirit fullness ignores this altogether. Rather than death to self, the Holy Spirit is seen as a means of promoting self. He becomes the means to my ends. He helps me to achieve my goals. He gives me a beautiful home.

While this may be true, any emphasis on the Holy Spirit simultaneously de-emphasizes self. We exist for Jesus Christ, not vice versa. The gospel is God centered, not man centered. To illustrate this further, how often have we heard something like the following:

- *The Holy Spirit is helping me to live without so many things I thought I had to have.*

- *The Holy Spirit is helping me to hold what has been for me a critical, judgmental tongue.*

- *The Holy Spirit makes me weary of my own duplicity.*

- *The Holy Spirit sensitizes me to the people and dynamics surrounding me.*

- *The Holy Spirit makes me nauseous of my old self and self-promotions.*

---

8. This quote is from Charles Inward, quoted by Pastor Alan Redpath in his sermon on the Holy Spirit (around 1981).

There's nothing glamorous or attractive about these things! But fullness does not happen apart from them. I must lose my life in order to gain it.

Popular teaching about the Holy Spirit emphasizes self. Biblical teaching about the Holy Spirit de-emphasizes self. If He is to live, then you must die. But remember: Resurrection power always and only follows a Calvary death. The decision seems clear, doesn't it?

CHAPTER 11

THE SECOND-HIGHEST
PRIVILEGE

*Today, many people are completely unfamiliar with even basic Biblical teaching.
We must follow the New Testament pattern for addressing a pagan culture.
(Chuck Colson)*

What is it? If we agree (and surely we do) that the highest privilege in life is knowing the Lord Jesus Christ, then the second highest must be sharing Him with others. Isn't this what we do on a solely horizontal level? We introduce our friends to our other friends. It is the most normal thing in the world. We have the high privilege of introducing others to Jesus Christ. When we do that, we are in fact evangelizing.

Do you remember the seminary professor I mentioned in an earlier chapter? One day in class he gave the following as a definition for evangelism: "Evangelism is telling what I know for sure about Jesus in the power of the Holy Spirit and leaving the results to Him." And every Christian can do that! Yet, it seems the excuses for not doing so are endless. So I want to ask a series of questions. I hope your answers to these questions will place in biblical perspective your privilege and responsibility to evangelize.

Have you ever thought about it? Every person you have known, know, or will know is eternal. Although earthly life will end, there is an eternity that will never end. Every person who has ever lived will spend forever in the unimaginable glory of heaven or the unimaginable horror of hell. This is what the Bible teaches.

Have you ever thought about it? I am responsible for my neighbor. My neighbor is the person next door or whomever the Lord crosses my path with. You may be the only contact they will have with the gospel. The gospel means good news. You have good news for them. If you were driving on an interstate at night and somehow discovered the bridge crossing a major river was out, you would not hesitate to flag as many oncoming cars as possible. It would be good news to them to hear about what was ahead and to avoid it. You see, most folks in our world don't know the bridge ahead is out. There is tragedy—and only tragedy—ahead for them. They must be warned. They must hear of another road. An alternative route. One that is safe and upon which they may safely travel. This is what we do when we evangelize.

Have you ever thought about it? Universalism is a lie. This heresy teaches that in the end, God will—after all—save everyone. Tragically, some Christians seem to believe this. The result is passivity and/or rationalization supporting their disobedience of non-evangelism.

Have you ever thought about it? Annihilationism is also a lie. This position says that even though there will be people in hell, their suffering will come to an end. They will be annihilated. This isn't true. Hell is as forever as heaven. The agony is indescribable and endless. John calls it a lake of fire (Revelation 20:10). Have you ever known a time when fire gave no light? It will be so in hell. Jesus called it outer darkness (Matthew 8:12). It never ends for those who are there. This is tragic. This is heartbreaking.

Have you ever thought about it? You will be in heaven soon. Safely home in the very presence of the Lord. But that arrival in heaven also means a discontinuation on earth. When my life on earth discontinues, then likewise my every opportunity to evangelize discontinues. I will have completed my race. This is why the scripture exhorts us that "Today is the day of salvation."

Today is when I make the overture. Today is when I visit. Today is when I ask questions. Might it be said of every Christian that they did their best to appropriate every opportunity to evangelize given them by the Holy Spirit.

Have you ever thought about it? After His resurrection, Jesus spoke of the Holy Spirit only in terms of power for evangelism (Matthew 28:18; Luke 24:47-49; John 20:21-22; Acts 1:8). This was pre-eminent on His mind. All the power of the world, flesh, and devil would be arrayed against His little apostolic band. Yet by promising and sending the Holy Spirit, His disciples would be indwelt with the greatest power of all!

It is true for you. You have the power of the Holy Spirit! If you are a Christian, you have Him indwelling you, but this power is for a specific purpose. It is to render you an effective and convincing evangelist. What our Lord commands, He gives.

It is a privilege as Christians to introduce men and women to someone who is greater than kings or presidents. It is to introduce them to the One who has made them for Himself. This privilege ends in heaven! So do it now, won't you? You neighbor is waiting.

CHAPTER 12

QUALIFYING AS AN EVANGELIST

Two hours and forty minutes after the Titanic struck the iceberg, she sank beneath the icy waters. Hundreds huddled in lifeboats and rafts, and others clutched pieces of wood hoping to survive until help came. For 50 terrifying minutes the cries for help filled the night. Eva Hart said, "The sound of people drowning is something I cannot describe to you. And neither can anyone else. It is the most dreadful sound. And there is a dreadful silence that follows it." Survivor Colonel Archibald Gracie called this, "The most pathetic and horrible scene of all. The piteous cries of those around us still ring in my ears, and I will remember them to my dying day."

During those final minutes a man drifting on a spar came within sight of John Harper. Harper, who was struggling in the water, cried, "Are you saved?" The answer returned, "No." Harper shouted words from the Bible: "Believe on the Lord Jesus Christ and thou shalt be saved." Before responding, the man drifted into the darkness.

Later, the current brought them back in sight of each other. Once more the dying Harper shouted the question, "Are you saved?" Once again he received the answer, "No." Harper repeated the words of Acts 16:31, "Believe on the Lord Jesus Christ and thou shalt be saved." Then the drowning Harper slipped into his watery grave. The man he sought to win put his faith in Jesus Christ. Later he was rescued by the S.S. Carpathia's lifeboats. In Hamilton, Ontario, this survivor testified that he was John Harper's "last convert."

Harper's last convert was won by Harper's last words, "Believe on the Lord Jesus Christ and thou shalt be saved."

There were many heroes on the Titanic, but, helping others as he drowned, John Harper was the last.[9]

I am using the word *evangelist* deliberately. While it is true that not every Christian has the spiritual gift of evangelism, it is equally true that every Christian has the responsibility. Anyone can sow seeds. Still there are basic qualifications necessary for every Christian who is obedient to our Lord's command to make disciples of every nation. I want to cite ten of these qualifications.

1. *I Must Be Born Again.* Jesus said so (John 3:7). I cannot give what I do not have. Life begets life. There are perhaps a significant number of people in our churches who are religious and good, but church life isn't divine life. Dead men can't share anything. The Bible declares the unsaved/ non-born again as dead (Ephesians 2). Clearly then, if I am going to share eternal life, I must have it. Do you?

2. *Assurance of My Salvation.* If I am tentative regarding the certainty of my salvation, then I will be significantly hindered in sharing it. There are those in the family of God who insist on one being able to specify day, date, time, and year regarding salvation. If this information is not given, then one's salvation profession is suspect. Personally I am able to recall a Sunday evening in San Diego in 1963 when I gave my life to Jesus Christ. I remember the speaker. I remember a man standing behind me who leaned over and asked me, "Do you want to go to the altar?" I don't know who that man was. We were visiting that church on that

9. Moody Adams, *The Titanic's Last Hero: A Startling True Story that Can Change Your Life Forever* (Greenville, SC: Ambassador International, 2012).

night. I was under conviction, but like young Samuel, had not yet come to recognize the Lord's voice (1 Samuel 3:7). The man standing behind me was led by the Lord. The Lord prompted me through him. I look forward to seeing him in heaven. I also remember my dad going to the altar with me. That night I became a Christian. Interestingly we lived in San Diego for only six months. We then moved back to my home state of North Carolina. A long way— east coast to west—for only six months, yet, I'll always be convinced that God moved us there just to save me!

Self-centered? Narcissistic? Someone special? Not at all. Just a humble and grateful realization of Acts 17:26-27. "From one man he made all the nations, that they should inhabit the whole earth and He marked out their appointed times in history and the boundaries of their lands. God did this so that they would seek Him and perhaps reach out for Him and find Him, though He is not far from any one of us."

So for me, I can say that I was born again on that Sunday evening. After that, there was one time—and only one time—when I seemed to doubt or lack assurance. It was some ten years later. I knelt by my bed and said very matter-of-factly to the Lord, "I believe I was saved ten years ago, but for some reason I am doubting. If it would please you Lord, whenever I stand back up on my feet, I would so appreciate this issue being settled." The Lord did assure me that I was His, that indeed I was saved, and now many decades later, that assurance stands.

However, we are reminded that Jesus did compare spiritual birth to physical birth. This was in His conversation with Nicodemus in John 3. Following then that particular illustration, we are reminded there are many in our world who have no record of their physical birth. The reasons are myriad: a third world country where such records aren't kept, or, where records were kept and were nonetheless destroyed by fire, war, earthquakes, and on and on. For that such person the question is not, *When was I born?* but rather, *What evidence is there that I'm alive?* Of course the ability to even ask the questions speaks of the presence of physical life. So we draw the parallel: Some Christians cannot remember the time and date of their conversion, so the question for them is, *What evidence is there of Jesus Christ living His life in me now?* Or to put it another way, they might say, *I'm simply not sure when I was born again, but I am sure of all the evidence I see within me, verifying that very act.*

This evidence is all throughout the New Testament: transformed thinking (Romans 12:1-2), fruit of the Spirit (Galatians 5), love for Jesus Christ (Matthew 22:36-40), obedience and purity (Romans 6), just to name a few.

Yes, it is imperative that you know with unwavering assurance that you are born again. Ask the Lord for this. He will show you. How deeply He desires that you rest and revel in His promises to save you (John 10:27-30). Then you can say with quiet calm and confidence, "I know what I have. I am sure, and I would be glad to tell you how you can also have this relationship with Jesus."

3. *Conviction Regarding Biblical Authority.* Apart from the Bible, we don't even know how to get saved. There is only one way, Jesus said, and that one way is described in the Bible (John 14:6). Furthermore, apart from the Bible, we don't even know how to live (Matthew 4:4). The Bible is invaluable. It is the Living Word—Jesus Christ—in written form, the Bible.

This Word was written by the Holy Spirit through the pens of men (2 Timothy 3:16; 2 Peter 1:21). It is absolutely authoritative. A Christian who is convinced of this will have the Bible as his or her final rule and authority for all of life, including every aspect of life. The Christian who does this is always mindful, in every situation, of some questions.

- What does God say about this?

- How does God feel about this?

- How does this make God look?

- How do I represent God in this?

We can always say that whenever the Bible speaks, God is speaking. Whenever God acts, He is always acting according—never contrary—to His Word. It is His self-revelation. We may even call it, reverently, an autobiography. It is a book about God, written by God.

In this book, He has made salvation so crystal clear. Likewise, He has made the consequences of rejecting salvation so very clear. A Christian who embraces the Bible as the very *breathed words* of God will have a deep and refreshing well of truth to draw from. He will have an unshakable foundation to stand upon. A biblical Christian is a powerful Christian. How perfectly this truth dovetails with the very theme of this book. We can say with absolute confidence that a Christian is never more filled with the Holy Spirit than when he or she is filled with the Word. These two always go together. They are complementary—to never separate from one another—so any talk of Spirit fullness apart from biblical depth is suspect. We can furthermore say that emphasis on the Spirit apart from the Word leans toward emotionalism. Emphasis on the Word, apart from the Spirit, leans to legalism. No. These two are wed together, the Spirit and the Word. Let no man therefore put it asunder.

4. *Purity of Life.* Purity is comprehensive. While sexual purity is certainly included, it is not exhaustive when it comes to speaking of purity in a believer's life. We are continually exhorted to cleanse or purify ourselves (2 Timothy 2:21; 1 John 3:3). A pure life is a sharp sword in the hands of the Holy Spirit. At this point I am including an excerpt from a pamphlet. It is one I have used for many years.

OMF International (formerly Overseas Missionary Fellowship) is the producer of this brochure titled, "O God, Revive Us Again: A Plan for Personal Revival."

Would you take time to pray through this? Ask the Holy Spirit to search your heart for any impurities that might be there. Keep a pure heart, dear one! Remember the promise that if you will, you will see God (Matthew 5:8).

Make a list of sins, shortcomings, failures, and impurities as revealed by Him, using the following suggested categories. "Basically, sin is the lack of conformity to the will of God as revealed in the Word of God. One kind of sin differs from another only in appearance and in intensity, not in character or essence."

A. Idolatry

(Matt. 6:33, 22:37) All things I have loved, sought or placed ahead of God: my work, family, pleasures, myself.

B. Rebellion

(I Cor. 10:10, I Sam. 15:22-23) All the sins I have committed against God, murmuring, rebellion, lack of submission to His will.

C. Self-Life

All the features and manifestations of the self-life. Here are some: a secret spirit of pride—an exalted feeling in view of your success, good training, appearance, (because of your natural gifts) abilities; an important, independent spirit, an attitude that says: "My way is the best, and I am always right." Love of human praise; a secret fondness to be noticed; love of supremacy; drawing attention to self in conversation; the stirring of anger or impatience, which you call nervousness or holy indignation; a touchy, sensitive spirit; a disposition to resent and retaliate when disapproved of or contradicted; a desire to fling sharp, heated words at another.

D. Self-Will

A stubborn, unteachable, spirit; an arguing, talkative spirit; harsh or sarcastic expressions; an unyielding and headstrong disposition; a driving commanding spirit; a disposition to criticize and pick flaws when set aside and unnoticed; a peevish, fretful spirit; a disposition that loves to be coaxed and humored.

E. Carnality

A man-fearing spirit; a shrinking from reproach and duty; a compromising spirit; a jealous disposition; a secret spirit of envy shut up in my heart; an unpleasant sensation in view of the success of another; a disposition to speak of the faults and failings, rather than the gifts and virtues of those more talented and appreciated than myself.

F. Dishonesty

A dishonest, deceitful disposition; the evading and covering of the truth; the covering up of my real faults; leaving a better impression of myself than is strictly true; false humility; exaggeration; straining the truth.

G. Unbelief

A spirit of discouragement in times of pressure and opposition; lack of quietness and confidence in God; a lack of faith and trust in God; a disposition to worry and complain in the midst of pain, poverty or at the dispensations of Divine Providence; an over anxious feeling about how everything will turn out.

H. Formality

Formality and deadness; lack of concern for lost souls; dryness and indifference; lack of power of God; love of ease and love of money. These are some of the traits which indicate a carnal heart (2 Tim. 3:1-5).

I. Service

All service, ministries, or activities that I do for my Lord that are substitutes for obedience, prayer and worship.

J. Worldliness

All the things in which I am not quite unspotted from the world, i.e., self-first, worldly pleasures, immodesty or vanity in appearance or dress. (Gal. 6:14; Jas. 1:27; I John 2:15-17; Matt. 6:24; 2 Cor. 6:16-18). Worldliness is thinking as the unsaved man thinks. (I, me, myself) rather than thinking and acting in accordance with God's will and his purpose for my life.

K. Lovelessness

All my sins against my neighbor—the way I have broken God's law of love toward Him (Jas. 2:8) resentment, criticism, impatience, deceit, unforgiveness (John 13:34-35).

L. Defeats

All hidden defeats that have not been revealed and dealt with (Heb. 4:12, 13; 2 Cor. 5:10; I Tim. 5:24).

M. Failures

All of my failures in real service as a winner of individual's souls, a discipler of others, my life of service, and more time in the Word and in prayer.

N. Snares

If there has been any contact with, or practice of the occult it must be repented of and forsaken; e.g., horoscopes, Ouija boards, occult magic, TV and movies based on occult, witchcraft, etc. (Deut. 18:9-12, 14; Gal. 5:19-21; I Sam. 15:22-23).

O. Miscellaneous

All that the Holy Spirit brings to my mind through the Word of God that does not seem to fit under the other categories (Gal. 5:16-25). Note the catch-all phrase in verse 21: "And such like," which includes all things that are not God-honoring or Christ-glorifying. Failing to do

*what God tells us to do in His Word is just as much sin
as doing what He tells us not to do (James 4:17).*[10]

I encourage you to reference this list often. The enemy is subtle and a great rationalizer. His job is to convince the Christians that their behavior isn't so bad after all—that God understands and will make allowances for you. No. Keep a pure heart. Remember that Jesus lives there by His Holy Spirit. You're the one to make sure the surroundings are made comfortable for Him. Rightly understood, the Lord Jesus Christ should feel perfectly at home in your heart.

5. *Spiritual Mindedness.* This is descriptive of how we think. How we think determines how we live. Behavior follows belief. Always. Jesus thought a certain way. He still does. That way is revealed in scripture. It is demonstrated through the Christian. When Jesus was looking, one day, at a crowd of people, He saw them a certain way. They were, to Him, as sheep without a shepherd. They were lacerated and torn. Matthew tells us that Jesus was moved with compassion (Matthew 9:35-36). This does not mean that He became emotional, necessarily. No. Something deeper was going on. To be moved with compassion is to have a physical sensation in the viscera. We would say that viewing those people was gut-wrenching for Jesus. A visual sight produced a physical result. He was spiritually minded. Does this happen to you?

In a mall, restaurant, or football stadium, where dozens to hundred to tens of thousands gather, do you see them as sheep without a shepherd? Heaven or hell bound? Lost or saved? You do if you are spiritually minded. This mindset is inevitable as we read the Word and pray. The transformation or metamorphosis spoken of in Romans 12:1-2 begins to take place. As I write these words, the current world population is over seven billion. All over the earth are different races, colors, and cultures. These are the nations

---

10. OMF International, from a brochure titled, "O God, Revive Us Again: A Plan for Personal Revival."

spoken of in scripture. In heaven there will be some from every nation, tribe, people, and language (Revelation 7:9). Men and women who think about these truths are indeed spiritually minded, and as a result of that, they will indeed go after the sheep who are without a shepherd. Will you?

6. *Love for People.* Love for people is the inevitable result of loving God. A cold, indifferent heart toward people is a cold, indifferent heart toward God (Matthew 22:36-40). I begin to love people by loving God. Be convincingly, irreversibly assured that Jesus does love the little children of the world. They are indeed precious in His sight. Many Christians seem to sit at home and think, *I don't feel anything for lost people, therefore I will not go.* But this is the wrong order. I want to feel before I go, but I promise you that if you'll go ahead and go out of simple obedience, your feelings will follow…sooner or later. Remember our last point? Jesus went before He felt. It is almost always the same for us. People can tell if we love them or not, and if we do, they will almost certainly open their hearts to us.

7. *A Basic Knowledge of All People.* Every person you and I meet—of every culture, age, socio-economic/educational status—all share commonalities. All,

- are created by and in the image of God,
- are persons of worth and value,
- are sinners,
- have questions and fears, and
- need a Savior.

It has been said that the ground at the foot of the Cross is level. That's true. Whosoever will, may come. No one is off limits. All will stand before Jesus Christ either as a believer or non-believer. Know these things. Be convinced of them. Then, as the Holy Spirit leads, cross any and every barrier to get to people.

Have you heard the story of the panic-stricken private who breathlessly told his commanding officer, "Sir, the enemy is everywhere. We are surrounded!" To which the officer replied, "Great! Let's not let one of them get away." Likewise we're surrounded by lost people. They are everywhere. Let's not let one of them get away.

8. *A Daily Devotional Time.* This is when and where we regularly come to the Lord in prayer and scripture reading. The plans for doing so are myriad. Prayerfully determine how the Lord is leading you. Set a start-stop time as far as possible. It is during these times we may expect the Lord to share His heart with us. I assure you the nations of the world are on His heart, and they will be on your heart as you listen to Him.

9. *A Sensitivity to Answered Prayer.* Simply put, watch for God to open doors after you've prayed. Commit each day to Him. He will arrange divine encounters. Perhaps the store clerk. Maybe a server in a restaurant. The possibilities are endless. It is rather futile to pray for opportunities to evangelize and then go about our business as if we hadn't prayed! Pray and watch!

10. *Spirit-Recognized Leadership in the Person-to-Person Encounter.* Once you sense God is opening a door with someone, how then do you proceed? Very often I will say to a waiter in a restaurant something like this: "My wife and I travel some and we always like to ask folks, Is there something we can be praying with you about?" You can usually tell a lot at this point and then decide where to go in the conversation. The Holy Spirit will lead you, but stay alert! Be warm and genuine. People can tell. Avoid being preachy or churchy. Jesus never was. If God has opened the door, then He's also prepared the one you'll be sharing with. Walk by faith. Be creative. Take the initiative. Open your mouth and speak! The Holy Spirit has given you a unique opportunity.

Also, rest in the Lord. The Coast Guard says, "We have to go out…we don't have to come back." It is the same with us. We do have to evangelize. We also are under orders, but we don't *have* to lead the other person all the way to faith in Jesus Christ. I hope you understand this. We are a link in a chain. Who except God knows what link we are or how long the chain is? We might be the very first person who has ever shared the gospel with someone. We might plant the first seed, or we might be the person who is present when the new birth occurs. All of this is up to the Holy Spirit. Our responsibility is obedience. We must do our part because He will not do it for us, and He must do His part because we can't do it for Him. Rest in this. Only Jesus saves. Stay sensitive to His Holy Spirit. He will lead you.

I have underscored ten qualifications necessary for effective evangelizing. How did you do? Now I encourage you to keep at it. I have tried to "keep at it" for many decades now. At times I've blundered badly. At other times every word seemed to find the right place. God is faithful, and He always honors obedience. He is an expert at hitting the bull's eye even with a crooked arrow. Trust each day to Him. Trust every word to Him. Some will respond. Some will not. But at least all will hear.

Recently my wife and I were sitting in an airport waiting for our flight. This particular airline had a spokesman poised by a kiosk. His job was to enlist the passers-by to sign up for that airline's credit card. This man was dauntless! He never slowed down. He never gave up! His overtures were very polite. "Good morning, Sir! Ma'am!" "Where are you flying today?" "Do you have a moment?" And so on. I estimated that about one in fifteen responded. He took that one aside, answered their questions, got them squared away, and then they went on their way. Immediately he was back at it! I observed him for about an hour. Absolutely consistent. What a great example and, frankly, no small indictment. He was fearless in promoting a credit card! The illustration is clear. The application is obvious. I hope it might be said of us—you, the one reading, and I, the one writing—that in evangelism, we were dauntless, consistent, and that we never gave up.

CHAPTER 13

A SUBTLE AND CONVINCING CAMOUFLAGE

Death is the supreme festival on the road to freedom. (Dietrich Bonhoffer)

This, of course, is the purpose of camouflage: to be subtle and convincing. Camouflage blends in. It isn't noticed. It appears natural. Camouflage is indispensable to the enemy's strategy of infiltration. That is true physically. It is true spiritually. I am identifying this subtle and convincing camouflage as the flesh: more specifically, the religious flesh.

Religious flesh is a camouflage. It feigns spirituality. It even purports Spirit fullness. It is extremely subtle...and effective, and it does seem that not a few in our churches have been duped by it. We must guard against it. Our vigil in doing so must be constant. Keeping the vigil means, first of all, asking the question, *What is Flesh?* The basic New Testament Greek word is *sarx* (pronounced like "sharks" but without the "h"). Although the New Testament draws some finer nuances of this word, I want to simply adapt two broad meanings for our purposes.

The first meaning of flesh is the physical body. This is essential to every human being. Every living person has a physical body. We should say, most accurately, however, that every living person lives inside their physical body. Our bodies are the dwelling place of, or the repositories for, our soul and spirit. At death, our bodies die when the soul and spirit leave or depart. We see this in the death of Jesus on the Cross. He first of all gave up His spirit and then died (John 19:30). His body was dead—completely. His spirit was alive—completely. It will be the same for us at our deaths. The flesh is defined in scripture as our physical bodies (2 Corinthians 10:3; Galatians 2:20). There is nothing wrong, sinful, or ungodly about our bodies. Jesus had one (John 1:14; Hebrews 5:7). It is what we do with our bodies that determines whether they are instruments of righteousness or unrighteousness (Romans 6:13).

Our bodies are, furthermore, where the Holy Spirit lives (1 Corinthians 6:19). Taking care of our bodies is a good, godly, and holy thing to do. I hope you will remember that. Take care of your body for Jesus' sake. This includes what I take into my body by way of eating; what I dwell on by way of thinking; what I communicate by way of speaking. We all have a body of flesh.

The second way scripture defines flesh is the unregenerate or unsaved man (Romans 7:5; 8:8-9). This speaks of the entirety of a lost person's modus operandi. Everything a lost person does is flesh, and because the flesh belongs to a person's old nature, then the flesh is always sin. What the Christian must remain ever alert to is the flesh. Furthermore, while most Christians understand the bad side of the flesh (stealing, murder, etc.), very few seem to understand how bad even the good side of flesh is.

In other words, there is reckless flesh and there is religious flesh. Paul had good religious flesh. He describes this in Philippians 3. In fact, his religious flesh was Grade A, but it is still flesh, and God hates all flesh! It is, in fact, hostile to Him (Romans 8:7), and those who are in the flesh cannot please God (Romans 8:8). I can sing hymns, pray prayers, and preach sermons all in the power of the flesh. Make no mistake! It is good, religious flesh, but it is worthless. All such endeavors will amount to nothing and will be burned up on judgement day (1 Corinthians 3:15; 2 Corinthians 5:10).

So how does a good, sincere, zealous Christian fall into this trap? For most of us the scenario goes something like this: We hear the truth preached, and we want to do it with all of our hearts, so we strike out with all of our human energy and ingenuity. We find people responding. They slap us on the back. They tell us how gifted, talented, and effective we are, and we believe them! But somehow, sooner or later, this all comes crashing down. I believe, frankly, this is the goodness of God intervening. He is saving us from ourselves! This crashing down is evidenced in burnout, sinful lifestyles, or just plain indifference/apathy.

The flesh cannot accomplish spiritual things. It can accomplish "churchy" things—not spiritual, however. I believe every Christian must come to this point. I believe every serious Christian will. The Holy Spirit is in this. He shows us our own shallowness, religious façade, playing to the crowd, religiosity, pharisaism, and more. In short, even though we are a Christian, we are shown quite unequivocally that we are bankrupt. The account we've been drawing from is empty. That bank is closed. Don't despair if you've come to this point. In fact, I hope you have. I hope you are desperately tired of yourself, your weak efforts, and your impotent Christian life. This is the key. Please remember that.

Some believers never get to this point. They love themselves more than they love Jesus. They love the accolades that come to their flesh rather than the less traveled road likely demanded of them by the Holy Spirit. They prefer the spotlight of religious cronyism rather than the darkness of the prayer closet. Unless they change, they have their reward in full. So the pressing question now becomes, *How does this change come about?* I believe we'll find transforming answers in Romans 6.

First of all, there are some things we need to know. Transformation results from revelation deliberately aimed at application. The Christian needs to know they died to sin (Romans 6:2), were baptized into Christ Jesus—into His death (Romans 6:3), and were buried with Him (Romans 6:4). Do you know these things? In the original language, "know" means recognizing, understanding. It even suggests the intimate relationship of a man and woman knowing one another. That is the right idea. We should be familiar with these truths to the point of intimacy. These are bedrock and foundational to living the Christian life in the power of the Spirit versus the power of the flesh.

We notice then about these four verbs that they are all past tense and all are passive. This means that something was done to us (we were passive), that it was done sometime in the past, and that "sometime" was over two thousand years ago at Calvary! The old spiritual asks, "Were you there when they crucified my Lord?" The answer is, Yes! Somehow we indeed died with Jesus Christ. We were baptized into His death. As we mentioned earlier in the book, to baptize is to immerse under. We were immersed into His death. This was all accomplished and superintended by the glory of God (Romans 6:4). This refers to His manifest presence. It also means that in the terrible, suffering, ignominy of the Cross, ultimately it was to the glory of God and the means of bringing many sons to glory (Hebrews 2:10). Dear one, this will not fit your logic. It is the perfect work of a perfect God. Even though we cannot explain this event logically, that doesn't mean we're ignorant. These, in fact, *are* things we can—indeed, must—know in order to live the Christian life the way our Father has designed it.

So now we know that two thousand years ago at Calvary and in the person of Jesus Christ, a co-death, co-baptism, co-burial, and ultimately a co-resurrection took place. God was in Christ, reconciling the world to Himself, and we were with Christ so that we could be reconciled and walk in a new life. This "new" described in Romans 6:4 means that which has never been before. In other words, we may go to a used car lot and buy a "new" car. While new to us, it isn't really new at all; it has "been before." Someone else has owned it. But the life we have as Christians is that which we've never had before. It is the very life of Jesus.

We are reminded of the words of the great hymn: "Morning by morning new mercies I see." These are things we need to know! Additionally, then, if we are committed to living the Christian life in the power of the Spirit versus the power of our flesh, there is someone with whom we must deal. It is our old self or old man (Romans 6:6).

This phrasing identifies every Christian before they were Christians. It is descriptive of who we were and how we thought. This old self was crucified with Christ. Spiritually speaking, that is a historic fact. It is the next sentence that sometimes confuses

Christians. It reads, "that the body ruled by sin might be done away with." The phrase means to be rendered powerless or to be put out of business. It is declared inoperative. So at this point, we must draw some conclusions:

1. The sin nature is not eradicated (if it were, we would never sin again).

2. Sin is not dead. Indeed, it is all around us.

3. We're not dead either.

4. But the relationship has been terminated! (See Romans 6:7.) We have been set free from sin.

To illustrate this, suppose someone is in the army for four years. While there, they had a demanding, intense commanding officer. Everything the officer commanded, the recruit *had to do*. But then the day came for an honorable discharge. The four-year veteran walks away from the military base, life, and commander. Then, suppose that commanding officer runs after him, yelling... screaming...ordering. Did you know that that newly discharged veteran no longer has to obey? Why? The former relationship has been terminated. The veteran is alive. The commanding officer is alive, but that former relationship is forever ended!

This is what happens when someone becomes a Christian. Sin will still shout, threaten, and demand, but because the Christian is now living in the power of the Holy Spirit, he/she may look at sin and say, "I can, but I don't have to." I must deal with this old man-self, but I no longer have to live his way. The relationship has been terminated. This is why the hymn says, "He breaks the power of cancelled sin." What does this mean? We may say it like this: when we are born again, God declares us justified (Romans 5:1). Justification therefore sets us free from the penalty of sin. What is that penalty? Death (eternal), judgement, and separation from God. When God justifies sinners, He is not declaring bad people to be good or saying that they are not sinners after all; He is pronouncing them legally righteous—free from any liability to the broken law because He Himself in His Son has borne the penalty of their law breaking.[11]

---

11. John R.W. Stott, *The Cross of Christ* (Intervarsity Press: Downers Grove, Illinois, 1986), 190.

We are answering the question, *What does "he breaks the power of cancelled sin," mean?* To justification, which frees us from the penalty of sin, we now add sanctification, which frees us from the power of sin. The Bible is clear: "Sin shall not have dominion over you, be your master" (Romans 6:14). Yet so many Christians would confess, "Indeed, it does!" They rationalize and try to reason away this sin control. They might say, *Well it isn't so bad. It is just a little sin. My daddy did it...guess it is okay if I do it. God understands. Jesus will forgive.* Of course they are deceived. Every time a Christian sins, he or she is believing a lie! Sanctification, then, is a lifelong work of the Holy Spirit in me, actively showing me how I can live with His power and help over the power of sin.

This is not sinless perfectionism. This is not "never sinning again," but on the other hand, the Bible is clear: for the maturing, Spirit-filled Christian, sin should be on an ever-decreasing frequency. He does set the prisoner free. Then we must say, finally, that one day there will be glorification. We will be in heaven. There we will be forever free from the presence of sin. Can you even imagine it? We've never been free from the influence and pervasiveness of sin. Our planet groans under the curse of sin. The devil entices to sin via demons, worldly philosophy, and the flesh. The Christian must stay on guard for all three.

We've been talking about how we as Christians may live no longer in the power of our religious flesh, but rather in the power of the Holy Spirit. We've said, (1) there are some things we need to know, and (2) there's someone with whom we must deal. Finally, (3) there is something we must do.

1. I must be aware of my own flesh patterns. Before I came to Jesus Christ, I had one way—and only one way—of doing things. This way became a pattern. Many Christians, however, even after coming to Jesus, still continue living by the old flesh patterns. Even though the old man was crucified, the flesh patterns were not. When I act according to these flesh patterns, I am living according to the flesh. This accounts for the carnal Christians in Corinthians (1 Corinthians 3).

    Rather than do that, however, I may now yield to the peaceful and princely life of Jesus living in me. He teaches me new patterns. As I read His Word, I begin to think differently. I find, then, I begin to carry myself differently! I'm a follower of Jesus Christ! I am a new creation!

I then find additionally that my flesh (both religious and reckless) becomes increasingly offensive to me. My flesh smells bad! It has a foul odor. This is to be expected. Paul calls it dung (Philippians 3). With this I find a hunger…even a desperation for the purity and attractiveness of Jesus in me and through me. My flesh seems so empty. He seems so grand! The choice seems so easy. I wonder why it took me so long.

2. I must choose to die. This choice is really an appropriation of my co-death, co-burial, and co-resurrection with Jesus. When I am instructed in Romans 6:12 to "not let sin rule over me," it sounds to me like I have a choice. And we do! I appropriate my death so that I may appropriate my resurrection. Resurrection power, only and always, follows a Calvary death.

3. I commit every moment to Jesus. Remember, I am walking in the Spirit. Walking is continual. I am living in the Spirit. This necessitates committing every moment to Him. "Lord Jesus, help me in this temptation"; "Help me to hold my tongue"; "Help me to recognize and choose your way." And so goes the Christian life: depending on, asking/ hungering for, and receiving His endless help.

In conclusion, stay alert to your flesh! It is convincing and conniving. It will whine, beg, and plead. It will assume the most religious posture you've ever seen! It will act respectable. Don't be deceived! Choose by appropriation to take your place with Christ Jesus on the Cross. Choose to die to sin and self. Ask His opinion/ evaluation of your life and ministry. He's the only one who sees and knows everything. Others may applaud you when He doesn't! Our religious flesh will look good to most people. Only a few are discerning enough to see through it. So receive compliments and plaudits genuinely…and yet prudently. Be ruthless with your own flesh, never sympathetic. The Holy Spirit is a faithful teacher at this point. He will capably point out flesh whenever/wherever He sees it.

He wants you to be richly rewarded at the judgement seat of Christ, which is called the *Bema* (2 Corinthians 5:10). Continue cultivating a sensitive heart to hear Him.

> *When George Muller, founder of the orphan homes of Bristol and often spoken of as the apostle of faith, was asked the secret of God's using him so mightily, he replied, "There was a day when I died." As he spoke this, Müller bent lower, until he almost touched the floor. He continued, "Died to George Müller, his opinions, preferences, tastes, and will; died to the world, its approval or censure; died to the approval or blame even of my brethren or friends; and, since then, I have studied only to show myself 'approved unto God'" (2 Tim. 2:15).*

> *How could George Müller trust God day by day for the food and all the expenses of two thousand people without ever advertising, ever asking for financial assistance, or ever answering people when they asked what his needs were? How could he carry this constant pressure without any sense of strain, without worry? Often his expenses were met one day at a time. He never had any reserve. Yet it was said that "the Twenty-Third Psalm was written in his face." The secret is that George Müller was crucified. Since he was truly crucified, the Holy Spirit could fill him and use him unreservedly.[12]*

---

12. Roger Steer, *A Living Reality: George Muller's Experience of God* (Hodder and Stoughton: London, 1985), 76.

CHAPTER 14

 # BROKENNESS

In order to break our wills to His, God brings us to the foot of the Cross and there shows us what real brokenness is. (The Calvary Road)

God uses broken things. We throw them away. It is, in fact, doubtful that God will ever use anyone significantly apart from brokenness. Scripture is replete with examples. Simply put, brokenness is the process whereby that which is on the outside is broken so that which is on the inside may be seen or expressed. In the case of the Christian, that which is on the inside is the Lord Jesus Christ. But, oh, the struggle sometimes in seeing Him! There seems to be so much in the way. Layer upon layer of self! Christianity is often humanism at its best. Humanism is when I am the center of my world. Everything is about me. Christianity is when Jesus is the center of my world. Everything is about Him.

I hope you've been tracking with me throughout these pages. I've been trying to say in as many ways as possible that the Holy Spirit will always promote Jesus Christ. He will always highlight Him. The Holy Spirit is not, first of all, about gifts, demonstrations, experiences, or emotions. All of these dynamics, however, will follow the Holy Spirit's ministry to a certain degree.

Brokenness facilitates that goal. Brokenness clears away all the subterfuge we as Christians tend to gather about ourselves. This might be seen in name-dropping, or talking about where I've been, or how much I'm doing for the Lord. It is a verbal resume! The goal is to impress. The objective is self-promotion. Sadly, the truth is that this sort of modus operandi is nothing more than my insecurities on display. When I'm insecure, then no matter what you bring to the table, what I bring to the table is always bigger and better. The truth is, I am not satisfied with Jesus while claiming all the time to be exactly that. Yet there is a better way! And even though costly, it is nonetheless so very settling and satisfying.

THE INTENT

What does the Holy Spirit have in mind as He initiates the process of brokenness? The intent is three-fold:

1. That Jesus Christ would be seen clearly, biblically, and authentically. The Christian life *is* Jesus Christ. He is alive not only in heaven but in the believer. A Christian witness is *not* one's best imitation of Him. It is Jesus, in the Person of the Holy Spirit, inhabiting and expressing Himself through the believer's voice, eyes, hands, feet, emotions. It is a present-day incarnation. The breaking process is to rid us of all the unnecessary luggage we've been carrying around. We don't need it! Jesus never tried to impress anyone. And we shouldn't either. Jesus alone is sufficient. The more we are broken from self-reliance and self-promotion, the more He is seen.

2. That the Fruit of the Spirit be seen (Galatians 5:22). What about you? Love, joy, peace, forbearance, kindness, goodness, faithfulness, gentleness, and self-control have always characterized Jesus. And they still do.

3. That the believer would be kept usable. This is critical. Some believers are very usable. They submit to the Potter's shaping hands. When those hands arrange, permit, or orchestrate circumstances, there's no whining or complaining. There is only an attitude that says, "According to Thy Word, let it be unto me." Mark it well: A Spirit-filled Christian is not a whiner! They are rather one who obeys the Word and gives thanks in all things because this is the will of God. If you are going

through a painful time in your life, I hope you will breathe a quiet, "Thank you, Father. You know what is best. Even though this experience is so very hard to bear, I thank You that You will never harm me and will, in fact, work this together for my good." You see, whatever you're facing is ultimately from the Father. Never mind the numerous second causes (people, the devil, physical issues); ultimately, our God rules and overrules. Nothing touches you without His permission. In all of His dealings with us—even the difficult ones—He is doing us a favor: He is keeping us usable.

ILLUSTRATIONS OF BROKENNESS

There are three illustrations on brokenness that I'd like to point to. I call these, (1) the breaking of the bread, (2) the breaking of the bottle, and (3) the breaking of the body.

The breaking of the bread is found in Matthew 15:32. The Gospels record two such supernatural events. There is the feeding of the five thousand—recorded in all four Gospels. Only Matthew and Mark, however, cover this event of the four thousand. Still, in every account there is a miracle. The bread available was woefully limited. The fish too. The disciples immediately began to figure the situation from the limitations of their own abilities: "Where could we get enough bread?" (Matthew 15:33).

This is indicative of an unbroken person. An unbroken person sees everything as depending on them, and sadly they will do this while declaring their faith in Him. This situation was deliberately ordained by our Lord. The disciples needed to see the impossibility. They needed to see that indeed, they could do nothing. Most of us think that we can do the small things. We need Jesus only for the big things. Yet, He said that apart from Him, we could do nothing. The disciples had no amount of cleverness or resources to handle this situation, but someone broken could! Hence, Jesus took the bread and fish and gave thanks. Afterwards, He broke these items. The result? Thousands ate and ate! There was even food left over! Jesus never runs out. His limitlessness however is limited by us. But it needn't be. Brokenness gives life. On that day, thousands of lives were sustained because of broken bread. It is a convincing picture of what Jesus will do through us. A limitless supply through a limitless Savior. This dynamic is intended to take place through every believer. But brokenness is the prerequisite.

We see then another illustration in *the breaking of the bottle*. It was an alabaster jar filled with perfume (Mark 14:3). Probably in the shape of a flask, this container would have been sealed and then necessarily broken open for its intended use. Most of us know this story well. We know for example that many Bible commentaries calculate the worth of this perfume as equal to a year's wages. But there it was. Poured out. Emptied in a matter of minutes. The expense—though fully understood by many—was still not too expensive for Mary. This is the point she illustrates. There is a cost to following Jesus Christ.

That cost varies with every believer. An unbroken person says, "No. The cost is too great. Risks too high. Unknowns too unknown." The broken person says a similar and yet dissimilar thing: "The cost *is* great. The risks *are* high. The unknowns *are* unknown; but count me in. The answer is *yes*." Which one are you, by the way? A broken person has consuming love for Jesus Christ. The giver of things is loved more than the things given. A broken person says, "Yes! I give this, I give that. What else can I give?"

Additionally, this act by Mary seems to show keen insight. An insight not very characteristic of the disciples. Jesus said that this action on Mary's part was connected to His yet future burial. The disciples always struggled with this. Someone has said that every time Jesus talked about His imminent death, the disciples changed the subject! So here Mary is anointing her Lord. This practice is normal in preparing dead bodies for burial. A physical, outward embalming. Yet, Mary does it while Jesus lives! Albeit He will only live a few hours after this event.

We draw insight from this incident. Broken people are discerning and perceptive. While fully in touch with their physical world, they, nonetheless, understand there is another world: the spiritual world. They understand the spiritual world controls the physical. The broken person doesn't make final decisions based on logic alone. The limitations of their five senses do not dictate what is possible. God alone decides this. Hence, Mary was not limited by logic or her five senses. Jesus was going to die. She had insight at that point and prepared for it.

But now in our third illustration, we come to very, very holy ground. It is *the breaking of our Lord's body*. This took place symbolically in the upper room. Jesus said the broken bread was His body. The disciples were to take and eat (Matthew 26:26). Just as the physical bread referenced earlier fed thousands, so now His death on the Cross would feed countless numbers throughout all the world and history. As the Living Bread, he would give the Bread of Life. This life was and is His very own: crucified, buried, and resurrected. A broken person understands this. They understand that resurrection power always and only follows a Calvary death. A broken person understands that one's cross is not a certain difficult person or circumstance. Lost, unregenerate people deal with these things also. Physical ailments, an obdurate mate, a certain temptation cannot be categorized as "one's cross to bear." No. A cross has always and only meant death. At the time when crosses were the normal form of execution, no one ever wondered what they were for. A man on a cross was dealing with one thing only: death. It is the same for the Christian. Death is not optional for the Christian. In fact, I cannot be one apart from taking up my cross and then getting and staying on it (Matthew 10:38; Galatians 2:20).

How this flies in the face of popular American theology! Innumerable books and media ministries aim at a better me! This position is a seismic shift from biblical theology. The scriptures teach that I exist for His purposes, not vice versa. His countless blessings have been abused. Instead of humbly receiving them, we have developed an entitlement mentality. We think He owes us. We've become spiritually soft, flabby, overweight, and lethargic. The idea of a cross is other worldly to many. It isn't convenient and doesn't fit their schedule. How unspeakably tragic this is. It grieves His great heart.

Yet, all of this notwithstanding, we must understand that if there is no Cross, there is no salvation. He died on the Cross to give it. We stay on the Cross, giving evidence that we have it. Do you?

Is this breaking process sounding more and more difficult? Less and less attractive? I hope you do not despair. There's no need to. Because there is something very special in being broken.

INTIMACY IN BROKENNESS

The Lord Himself is strategically involved in brokenness. This should greatly encourage you.

1. Brokenness is always in tender love. The Bible says that our God will never stop doing us good (Jeremiah 31:40). Then again, He declares His everlasting love for us (Jeremiah 31:3). To put it another way, our Father treats us like He treats His Son because we are in the Son. An indissolubility exists between the Christian and the Savior. Furthermore, we are sons by adoption. Breaking is for our good. Learning to distrust self is an education money can't buy. It is through us, not by us, that God does His work and Jesus lives His life. Those little prepositions spell the cataclysmic difference between the Christian life as the Bible defines it or the Christian life as we define it. The issue is not first of all what we do as Christians, but rather the source of our doing. It is flesh or Spirit. For the broken person, it is Spirit.

2. God always sets limits on the process. He ceases the present breaking process when to continue doing so would damage rather than promote His purpose for our lives. He is the refiner, sitting by the fire (Malachi 3:3). He never makes a mistake. The temperature is never too hot. Remember: He will never stop doing you good.

3. Brokenness is designed to produce a teachable spirit in us. Psalm 119:71 says, "It is good for me to be afflicted so that I might learn your decrees." Whenever, wherever you find a teachable Christian, you know at least one thing about them. They're broken. The Word of God does get through to them. He is not fighting His way through layer upon layer of flesh, self, carnality, religion, churchianity, self-importance, and more. No. They've been broken from all that. There is nothing in the way. They know it, and the Father knows it. They delight to do His will. Anyone can! Teachable people are broken people. It is a comparatively small price to pay when compared to the wealth received.

God uses broken things. He never throws them away. Broken people make the most significant difference eternally, and they are making the most significant difference now.[13]

---

13. The author was first introduced to this teaching on brokenness by Pastor Paul Burleson at Southcliff Baptist Church, Ft. Worth, Texas, 1981.

CHAPTER 15

BROKENNESS FOR THE SAKE OF OTHERS

Those who have been gripped by the power of the Holy Spirit and are used for God's glory are those who have been broken in their finances, broken in their self-will, broken in their ambitions, broken in their lofty ideals, broken in their worldly reputation, broken in their desires, and often broken in their health. Yes, He uses those who are despised by the world and who seem totally hopeless and helpless, just as Isaiah said: "The lame will carry off plunder."

(Isaiah 33:23; Streams In The Desert)

I t is vital to be broken. Potential blessing for countless numbers is contingent upon it. Some of the conclusions and dynamics that we will ultimately see in heaven hinge on your brokenness now. Brokenness, we remember, is the very life of Jesus residing on the inside of the Christian, coming through the Christian, and touching the world all around the Christian.

Jesus is Lord over the entirety of the Christian: body, soul, and spirit. How does this work itself out practically? We recognize first of all that man is a trichotomy, not a dichotomy. A threesome versus a twosome. A tricycle rather than a bicycle. We are body, soul, and spirit. Our body is our physical structure. Our soul is our inward structure. It consists of mind, will, and emotions. The Greek word is *psuche* (pronounced "soo-kae"). This is the root of our word *psychology*. Thirdly, we are spirit. This is our innermost being. Thus, body, soul, and spirit. The apostle Paul affirms this in 1 Thessalonians 5:23.

Everyone on the planet has a body, soul, and spirit. However, the spirit remains dead in trespasses and sin until one is born again. This accounts for Paul's declaration in Ephesians 2:1. Reading this, we conclude that at one time the Ephesian Christians were dead. Even so, they were alive in body and soul. Thus, they could function, discourse, and associate with others in the living of life. Their bodies worked. Their souls worked. But their spirit was dead! Thus, they had no ability to relate to God. This was fulfillment of the Lord's word to Adam in Genesis 2:17: "But you must not eat from the tree of the knowledge of good and evil. For when you eat from it you will surely die." We know that Eve and Adam did eat and, in fact, did die. But what died? Not their bodies—at least not then—nor their souls (mind, will, and emotions). It was their spirit that died: their innermost being. God was gracious and provided a blood sacrifice for their sin so that they might continue to have a relationship with Him (Genesis 3:21).

Yet because of Adam and Eve's sin, every person born since then has inherited a sin nature. There are no exceptions. Furthermore, we can conclude that because of the indwelling sin nature, most of the world is only two-thirds alive. Men and women are alive in body and soul but dead in spirit. When we take all of this and apply it to the Christian life, we begin to understand why some Christians never seem to grow...while others grow exponentially. The reason is many Christians, after having their spirit resurrected and made alive at salvation, nonetheless, still live the Christian life physically and soulishly only. They live by virtue of their minds—what they think, their wills—what they want, and their emotions—what they feel.

Since the soul (invisible) resides within the body (physical), the body is also involved in the futile and frustrating effort to live the Christian life. My body responds to the dictates and commands of my soul. If my mind, will, and emotions are afraid to evangelize, then my body will not go! Likewise, if my mind, will, and emotions are governed by circumstances verses God's truth, then my body will not go to church or fast and pray or deny itself anything. These dynamics characterize soulish Christians. They are everywhere and wreak no small havoc in the local church. Their Christian growth is desperately stunted. They try to live the Christian life from the standpoint of their soulish efforts. Miserable.

When, however, a Christian is broken, they no longer come under the authority of the physical and soulish. We may envision the Lord Jesus Christ, in the Person of the Holy Spirit, taking up His headquarters in our spirit! This becomes the base of His operations. Now, from the standpoint of our innermost being—our spirit—He exercises authority over our entire being: body *and* soul! My body doesn't tell me what to do. My soul isn't in control either. It is the Holy Spirit spreading, if you please, His holy umbrella over everything I am.

Because I've been willing to be broken from any and all dependence on self, I am now fully dependent upon Him. I live life and make decisions based on *one thing alone*: What is the truth? What does God say about this or that? My soul will often protest. My body will be petulant and childish. But those portions of my being aren't in control. He is! I, then, see all things as they relate to truth. In other words, we are often tempted to see truth through circumstances. That is, the circumstances are clear—black and white. The truth seems gray and far away. A broken person, however, sees circumstances through truth. It is the truth that is clear—black and white. The circumstances, though real, are not what determine my course. Truth does.

A broken person is freed from living by the soulish or physical. To the contrary, there is now unanimity in our human trinity of body, soul, and spirit. There is symmetry. This is why I've said it is vital to be broken. So many are affected—positively—by our brokenness.

We see this dynamic illustrated even further on any given Sunday morning. Take for example the Christian who, although their spirit has been resurrected, nonetheless continues living from the standpoint of the physical and soulish. When they listen to a sermon, their bodies are certainly involved. They see the preacher and hear the sermon. Their mind, will, and emotions, however, may be somewhere else. Because of that, all they walk away with is information. Their physical ears have heard the preacher's audible voice. Nothing has happened beyond that.

Now take that same person and add the dynamic of their souls. At this point, what they think, feel, and will is involved in what they hear. They are engaged, listening and processing. In the best-case scenario, they are inspired by what they hear. Their mind, will, and emotions have been reached. To the mere information received, only by their ears we may now add inspiration.

However, this is as far as it goes. There's no appreciable change. Their Christian life remains on the horizontal. As the saying goes, *a mile wide, but only an inch deep*. Many Christians are stuck here. Faith seems unrealistic. Prayer seems perfunctory. This Christian is a soulish Christian. They are indeed tossed about. Many sincere Christians just continue on in this sort of spiritual agony. But now add the third dynamic of the spirit. A broken person lives on a spiritual level. This is the level of truth. In the most difficult circumstances, there is consistency. In the deepest heartache, there is a simple trust in the Father who never makes a mistake. Being spiritual isn't being churchy. It is being normal! This person hears the preacher's words in their inmost being. There, by faith, it is received, grasped, and applied. Now the listener has not only information and inspiration; they have transformation. This is the whole idea, isn't it? This doesn't cancel out the intellect. It doesn't ignore some very hard theological questions. Indeed, brokenness facilitates those issues. It throws us hard on the Holy Spirit, crying out for discernment and insight. Brokenness teaches us that the *only* way to live life fully is to do so by faith. Yes… this does require humility. Pride is the single greatest factor inhibiting brokenness. Humility is the single greatest factor promoting it.

A broken person is easily identifiable. Their posture, countenance, words, tone, responses, and even body language all speak of another life indwelling. It is the life of the Lord Jesus. And now, just as when He was on the earth, He continues to impact everyone who comes in contact with Him. He does that through the Christian. This is why it is so vital that you be broken. Potential blessing for countless numbers is contingent upon it.

Our Old Testament example for all of this is Moses. His story begins in Exodus 3. You probably already know this story; yet, doesn't it strike you as unusual, at least, that an eighty-year-old man is asking, "Who am I?" (Exodus 3:11). It is a strategic question. For every Christian, it is a priority question. We all already know about ministry. Each Christian has one or more. Our ministries and callings are commensurate with our gifting, talents, and temperament. But our first question is not one of ministry. It is one of identity.

IDENTITY

Every Christian knows "whose they are." Many, however, don't know who they are. The question has to be answered. Often times a Christian may believe themselves to be this or that: a spouse's expectations; a parent's expectations; a church's expectations. They have sacrificed themselves to someone else's mold. That mold hardly ever fits. God has a mold that will fit. At eighty years of age, Moses was beginning to find his. The answers given him by the Lord were three-fold. His identity was seen first of all in sanctification. The Lord, by His answer, seems to have not even heard the question asked by Moses, "Who am I?" The expected answer might be, *You are the son of Jochebed*, or, *You are a Hebrew*, even possibly, *You're Pharaoh's adopted son*.

SANCTIFICATION

The Lord bypasses all of those natural answers. Instead, He simply says, "I will be with you" (Exodus 3:12). This is sanctification. It is belonging to the Lord exclusively. Moses' identity from then on was inextricably tied up in and inseparably with God. A whole new dynamic had begun for Moses. He was not his own. He was the Lord's.

In this we see that how a leader sets himself apart to the Lord affects significantly how followers set themselves apart to the Lord. Employees follow employers. Fathers affect their children. The pews follow the pulpit. Truth must first affect me if it is going to affect those around me. The Holy Spirit indwells every Christian. They are, then, by definition holy or sanctified. However, this identification may only be positional, not practical. I can be holy and not live holy. That's a sad truth every Christian has experienced. Or, I can be holy and live holy. That's also a truth every Christian can experience.

Separation

The second aspect of identity involves separation. These two words (sanctification and separation) can be identical in meaning. I want, however, to draw ever so slight a distinction. We may say it like this: *In sanctification, I set myself apart to the Lord and His ways. In separation, I separate myself from me and my ways.* Exodus 2:12 is very different from Exodus 3:11. We see Moses' agenda in 2:12. The Lord's is in 3:11.

In Exodus 2:12 Moses is in charge. In Exodus 3:11 the Lord is in charge. It is clear that Moses had been undergoing the breaking process. That particular subject took forty years to understand, and the subject was taught in the classroom of the desert! Don't despair, dear reader, if you're in the desert. It might be one of the best things the Father has ever done for you! There He can teach you. Solitude is an unsurpassed teaching method. I believe frankly that a maturing Christian has a deepening affinity for the desert. Lonely? Desolate? Barren? No question. Yet there is a fellowship that is sometimes experienced in no other way. This attitude and practice of separation becomes a powerful tool in the Lord's hands.

Speech

A third aspect of identity is speech. We see this in Exodus 4:12. There the Lord says to Moses, "I will help you speak and will teach you what to say." We have already noted this as an initial evidence of Spirit fullness, and, of course, it can't be over emphasized. We've all known the sinking heart feeling that comes whenever we misspeak. Worse still, Jesus doesn't call it misspeaking. He says that indeed our words have come right out of our hearts (Matthew 12:34). What a hard truth this is to digest. An indifferent Christian my respond, "Oh, well, you know what I meant." While this is often true for a married couple or close friendships, I'm speaking of something different from that.

A broken person is ever keen to the Spirit within and the surroundings without. This person is learning how to speak a word in season. They are learning when not to speak at all. They are not nervous with the communication of quietness. They frankly have no compelling need to speak at all! Jesus was and still is the master of everything. He teaches us how and when to speak, just as Moses learned. So may I ask you, *Are you speech conscious?* This is not living under a legalistic oppression, ever fearful of saying the wrong thing. To the contrary, there is a great rest in the Lord. I am learning to trust Him. I am learning the quiet confidence that whenever I open my mouth, I may depend on His voice being heard.

This is the increasing experience of every broken person. Their tongue is controlled by the Holy Spirit. This is no small miracle! Biblical identity, then, is pivotal in the Christian life. I'm not what or whom I used to be. I am not necessarily what others expect me to be. I am, rather, discovering and growing in who God says I am. I rest in this, knowing that it is His opinion that matters the most.

STRATEGY

Following identity, wherein God wants the Christian to know who and whose they are, there is the dynamic of strategy, wherein God wants the Christian to know how He does His work.

At this point, God informs Moses that He will deliver Israel out of the hands of the most powerful army on earth. This was certainly agreeable to Moses. We recall that he had already attempted this forty years earlier (Exodus 2:12) with the very obvious strategy of an unbroken man. Moses' prowess, however, and high standing in the Egyptian community were not the tools God intended on using. To the contrary, there must be with Moses, and us, a healthy distrust in all things flesh. So the first thing God teaches Moses is that He does the supernatural through the ordinary. For Moses, this meant the so very basic and perfunctory ordinariness of a shepherd's staff, his own physical hand, his tongue (already mentioned), and his brother Aaron (a concession he probably regretted later; Exodus 32:1-5, 22-24).

God was going to do the supernatural through the ordinary. This is always so! Those believers who are unaware of this truth simply opt to accomplish only the ordinary through the ordinary. Their lives, in other words, *can* be explained. This was not so with Moses. There simply was no explanation for what Moses did apart from God. It can be and should be the same with us. Now think for

111

a moment: are you facing anything as formidable as the Egyptian army? You may think so. At the very least, you're most likely facing something requiring much, much more than you have. That is the point. So the question is, *What do you have?* You have a God-crafted opportunity to see God do the supernatural through the ordinary. It may or may not be of Red Sea proportions. It doesn't matter. God's work is always supernatural simply because it is His own power and life at work.

Some would testify that the Lord gave them a forgiving heart. Others have known incredible peace when everything surrounding them was tumultuous. The supernatural doesn't have to be sensational. Jesus isn't some vaudeville side show obligated to titillate our religious flesh. But, oh, how deeply He desires to reveal Himself to and through us. When this happens, the supernatural is seen through the ordinary. Always. This is the sweet reality known to every broken Christian. They are convinced of their ineptness. They not only know their need, they gladly acknowledge it. They've already tasted the futility of the best laid plans of mice and men. Their very best efforts, like those of Moses, have often interfered with, rather than facilitated, the Lord's work. Brokenness in them is working. They are continuing to be usable.

The second lesson God taught Moses about strategy was as profound as the first. Namely, God uses our weakness, not our strengths. We can accomplish *our* work in *our* strength. We can't accomplish *God's* work in *our* strength. The outstanding illustration of this is King Nebuchadnezzar in Daniel 4. His very words were, "Is not this the great Babylon I have built as the royal residence by my mighty power and for the glory of my majesty?" (Daniel 4:30). That statement cost him his sanity, which God graciously returned to him. The restoration took place when Nebuchadnezzar looked toward heaven. After this he praised the Lord rather than himself (Daniel 4:34-37). Weakness…not strength. Incredibly (and seemingly) a great number (probably most) of the people God uses are indeed strong. This is true for the Old Testament, New Testament, and the church age as well. Likewise, for them God has set in motion the breaking process. They were powerful men and women indeed. Still, it was His strength at work in their weakness.

This is a huge problem for Christians in the American church. It seems we make every effort possible to suggest to others our strengths, our having-it-togetherness, and our ready answers for any and all questions. We demonstrate this by the cars we drive, clothes we wear, theological jargon we use, and homes we live in. The Jones have nothing on us. In fact, we've excelled way beyond that used-to-be standard. Fifth Avenue capitalism is alive and well in the American church. We can be as materialistic as our pagan neighbors. A broken person has no desire—even less, need—to fabricate or embellish the truth. A broken person is okay if others think they are weak. A broken person understands at the organic level they have nothing to prove and no need to impress.

Moses was an incredibly strong personality who became weak. He discovered that God deliberately uses weak things. Dear reader, everyone has weaknesses. These are not sins but weaknesses. Could I encourage you to stop trying to be strong? Stop trying to be in control? Stop trying to intimidate or influence others by where you've been or whom you know. Be yourself! Be weak in yourself. Be strong in the Lord! God uses people just like you to change the world.

I hope you've been encouraged so far. I hope you've been challenged. Maybe you've been surprised at times. Maybe you've already known most of what I've been saying. It has all been purposeful. It has all been moving toward one place. That place is worship. We see this in Exodus 4:29-31. This is the constant in every broken person.

MINISTRY

We call this third dynamic *ministry*. This follows identity and strategy. In the case of ministry, we find that God wants the Christian to know their purpose. Their purpose is to be a catalyst God uses to *draw others to worship*. God wants to do that through you. He indeed will do it through you if you are broken.

I hope you didn't just run past the last couple of sentences. In case you did, let me say it again: *Your purpose is to be a catalyst God uses to draw others to worship.* You've probably never envisioned yourself as a worship leader, yet the truth is that the Holy Spirit is the only true worship leader. He is always turning our attention to the worthiness and majesty of Jesus Christ. A broken Christian has nothing in the way to prevent that. When men and women are around them, there is an awareness of Jesus Christ. This is not superficial or a preachy, religious put on. It is the presence of Jesus Christ in the believer. The religious decorations that once adorned them are gone. Pious platitudes are missing from their lips. The living Lord is seen authentically and convincingly.

The Israelites bowed down and worshiped (Exodus 4:31). This event almost certainly means less to us than it truly should. Whenever you and I hear the word *worship*, we usually envision a certain place and a certain hour. For we who are living in the West that means, additionally, a temperature-controlled room, cushioned seats, proper lighting and acoustics, and in an increasingly casual culture, sandals, shorts, and coffee. Do you see this? This style of worship is all about me. My delight is not in Him (as all true worship is) but rather in the accouterments of worship. Every Christian who is committed to true worship must ask himself, *Can I worship apart from all the externals?* The Israelites did!

We draw a significant conclusion from this: worship is never dependent upon circumstances. The conditions surrounding the Israelites were such that we can't even imagine. The word *slavery* (which was the current condition of the Israelites) means almost nothing to us. We can define it while still not understanding it. Worship never depends on feelings, surroundings, or comfort. It depends on the faithful Holy Spirit who demonstrates the Lordship of Jesus over all of these vacillating circumstances. In fact, it could be said, furthermore, that if I am not worshipping in the extreme adversities of life, then almost assuredly, I'm not truly worshipping when conditions are optimal.

Our brother Job is the convicting illustration of this. Upon receiving news of the tragic death of his ten children, he "fell to the ground in worship" (Job 1:20). The Israelites did this. There is no record of them having done this before. This makes it seem all the more remarkable at first. But really, not so. They had what we have. Only we have much more! They had the truth of God's Word (4:30). So do we. They had some knowledge of God. The name by which

God identified Himself to Moses (4:15) was Yahweh (pronounced "yah-way"). It is the name used most often in the Old Testament for God. It is the name that illustrates His covenant nature. God had made a covenant with Abraham. Covenants are binding. God does not forget what He has promised. Every usage of Yahweh reaffirms this.

Furthermore, Moses writes that the Israelites heard that the Lord (Yahweh) was concerned about them and visited them (Exodus 4:31). This Hebrew word describes action on the part of God that produces a beneficial result for His people. The result of these dynamics (hearing the truth and a knowledge of God) was worship. The Christian has these dynamics ultimately. We have a complete Truth, both written and living. The written Truth is the Bible. The living Truth is Jesus. In the free world, we have the written Word available to us. In the restricted world, believers have only the Living Word available. He alone, then, is sufficient for worship. This, then, is the Christian's purpose. It is, likewise, the inevitable result of brokenness.

Moses was the outstanding Old Testament leader. Yet it is not by adjectives or superlatives that we describe him, rather it is by brokenness. It was a lesson he would continue learning for the next forty years. Yes, brokenness does cost you something. I hope you are willing. I hope you will come under whatever circumstances God requires of you. We throw broken things away. God uses them. He uses broken people. He uses broken churches. Some resist and thereby determine their minimal use by God. Others submit, and their lives are explainable only in terms of God. Which one will you be?

CHAPTER 16

JONAH:
THE MAN WHO WAS
NEVER BROKEN

The absurd man is he who never changes. (Auguste Barthélémy)

I s the truth of brokenness beginning to make sense to you? No—
actually, I said that wrongly. The truth is, brokenness absolutely
does not make sense unless you're broken. Biblical brokenness is
not like our cultural brokenness. Our culture loathes broken things.
They are useless. A scrap heap, junk yard, or an already overcrowded
garage is where we put broken things. But we have to learn to think
differently. God isn't like our culture. His evaluations are different.
He deliberately sets the process of brokenness in motion. He
deliberately—and significantly—uses broken people. Circumstances,
pressures, calamities, misunderstandings, and perplexities are just
a few of the God-sent, permitted dynamics intended to foster
brokenness. Frankly, this is *not* the sort of Christian life we see or
hear presented through much of Christian media. Not a few of the
Christian talk shows tout a Christian image that would challenge

anything Hollywood has to offer. The sad thing is this is nothing more than marketing. The rich and the famous grace the covers of books, celluloids of DVDs, and platforms of churches. A ripped up, torn, bloodied, emaciated, exposed body on a tree can't compete with that, and tragically, it seems that not very many care.

The counter to all of this Christian Disneyland gobbledygook is brokenness. Authenticity rings true in a broken person. Showmanship is anathema to a broken person. However, from all of what I have said in the last few chapters, it is still possible to remain unbroken; to remain in the driver's seat; to remain the hot shot; to remain the big *me*! Although almost unbelievable, this is exactly what Jonah did. As far as the Bible is concerned, he was never broken. Does it not strike you with incredulous irony that Jonah isn't even mentioned in Hebrews 11? That great "Hall of Faith." Think about it: Jonah preaches and some one hundred twenty thousand are saved (Jonah 4:11). Compare that to Noah. He preached for one hundred twenty years and only eight were saved (Genesis 6:3; 7:7). Yet it is Noah, and not Jonah, who is listed in Hebrews 11! As I said, God isn't like our culture. So then, let's take a few minutes to learn from our brother Jonah.

We'll be careful to note that we shouldn't do some of the things he did—and at times, we should do the things he didn't. We know first of all that Jonah resisted brokenness. We know he resisted because he refused God's truth (Jonah 1:2-3). There was no misunderstanding on Jonah's part. God's message was absolutely clear: "Go to the great city of Nineveh and preach against it" (Jonah 1:2). Upon hearing this perfectly clear directive, Jonah literally and deliberately went in the opposite direction (Jonah 1:3). In so doing he refused God's truth. As I mentioned early on in this book, Jonah couldn't/wouldn't embrace the truth. Namely, God was for the Gentiles: the non-Jews. Jonah was therefore to discover that truly no man is an island. His prejudice against the Assyrian pagans was not something he could contain. It began leaking out while still on his rebel boat ride. I hope we can get our arms around this: everyone on board was affected—almost fatally so (Jonah 1:4-16).

Imagine! An entire ship, cargo, and crew, all about to drown, all because of one man: God's man—on the run from God. It is almost paralyzingly somber to me to think how my decisions as a

Christian can affect so many. A broken person is aware of this. An unbroken person (Jonah) doesn't care. Jonah was the president of his own fan club. Jonah was looking out for Jonah. An unbroken person always does. A broken person understands that you should always obey God, no matter the cost, and leave the consequences to Him. An unbroken person always plays it safe. His contingency plans are endless. It has been said that the current generation of Christians in America is the *only* generation that has concluded, "If risk is involved, God can't be in it." Somehow, we've come to believe that *our* safety is the most important thing. This sort of belief is frankly unbelievable! It has *never* characterized our Christian history and heritage. Our past is a bloody one. Just ask the martyrs. Mark it well: no matter the cost/risk of obedience, the cost/risk of disobedience is greater— always. The following testimony bears witness:

> *I'm risking a lot, but it is more important to be obedient to God than to be worried about safety. It is more important to be attentive to what God says and what God is doing in our lives and to seek wisdom from Him in every step we make to spread the gospel. That is the safest place to be. (Open Doors Newsletter, August 2016, Pastor Murat, Central Asia).*

So Jonah disobeyed. He refused God's truth. I hope you do not do this. I hope you are hungry for, not casual toward, the truth. I hope your food (John 4:34) is to do the will of Him who sends you. I hope you are becoming more and more familiar with the Word. I hope you regard the men and women of scripture as your brothers and sisters. I hope you are being renewed in your mind. I hope your response to every situation is, *What does God say about this? What is the truth here?* Learn from Jonah. Do what he didn't do. Hear the Word and do it! Yet remarkably, God wouldn't let Jonah go! You know the story: God appoints a whale. Jonah is swallowed by the whale. Jonah prays while in the whale (Jonah 2). How one's imagination runs here! Was he consumed with the smell of dead fish? Or overcome with the gaseous odors of the whale's belching? How did he stay afloat in that slippery wet place? Did he ever stop praying for those three days? Nights? Would you? Suffice it to say, Jonah's circumstantial whale was custom designed just for him by a holy God. And yes, you can count on it; there is a custom-designed, circumstantial whale with our name on it, just waiting. The way to avoid it is through obedience.

We, for the most part, are rather indifferent about disobedience. After all, Jesus will forgive, right? But God is more serious about it than we can imagine, and He is more serious about His relationship with us than we can imagine. He pursued Jonah as much, or more, than He pursued the Ninevites. Jonah was valuable to God—unspeakably so. God therefore commands the whale to vomit Jonah on dry land (Jonah 2:10). Having thus been unceremoniously ejected, Jonah "obeyed the Word of the Lord" (Jonah 3:3). Nineveh does repent, and God does not "bring on them the destruction He had threatened" (Jonah 3:10).

All of this brings us to a conclusion and a question. The conclusion is, God used Jonah even though he was unbroken (this is clear in Jonah 4). The question is, *Why all the fuss about brokenness?* After all, Nineveh is saved. Jonah obeys. All's well that ends well. Isn't that right? No. I wonder...

- What if God had further assignments for Jonah? While none are mentioned, I have no doubt that Jonah's petulant attitude actually made him less, not more, usable.

- What about Nineveh?

Ultimately, this capital city of Assyria changed its mind regarding both God and His people. As an invasionary force in 722 BC, they virtually decimated the ten northern tribes of Israel. What if Jonah's heart had really been broken? What if he had had pity on the Ninevites? What if he had stayed and discipled them? These questions are speculative. They have no answer but must be asked. We know for sure that a broken Jonah would have been far more usable than an unbroken one. So his story concludes in Jonah 4. He's angry with God for saving the Ninevites. Proving himself to be only a mediocre servant, he decides to become a botanist. He became delighted in a plant, disgusted with people. No maturity. A little ministry, a whole lot of misery. This is Jonah's legacy. He was a man who was never broken. This is a hard lesson, don't you think?

But it is still a necessary one. Brokenness is a choice. It is one of God's changeless ways. I hope you will submit to it.

I want to close this chapter with the following quote. It is very helpful, and I hope you identify with it.

> *The great weakness in the North American church at large, and certainly in my life, is our refusal to accept our brokenness. We hide it, evade it, gloss over it. We grab for the cosmetic kit and put on our virtuous face to make ourselves admirable to the public. Thus, we present to others a self that is spiritually together, superficially happy, and lacquered with a sense of self-deprecating humor that passes for humility. The irony is that while I do not want anyone to know that I am judgmental, lazy, vulnerable, screwed up, and afraid, for fear of losing face, the face that I fear losing is the mask of the imposter, not my own!*
>
> *If there is a conspicuous absence of power and wisdom in the North American church, it has arisen because we have not come to terms with the tragic flaw in our lives: the brokenness that is proper to the human condition. Without that acknowledgment, there can be little power, for as Jesus said to the apostle Paul, "My power works at its best in your weakness" (2 Cor. 12:9).[14]*

---

14. Brennan Manning, *Ruthless Trust* (New York: HarperSanFrancisco, 2000), 122.

CHAPTER 17

THE HOLY SPIRIT AND PRAYER

Those who pray shape history.

Have you ever arrived late to a public prayer meeting? You open the door and find heads bowed, voices softened, and there is the sense that heavenly business is taking place. However, when we're late, we're at a distinct disadvantage. We've missed all which has led up to that point. What burdens of the heart have been shared? What truths from the Word have been taught? How has the Holy Spirit directed that meeting right up until the time of prayer? It is very important to know those things if I am to enter into the spirit of prayer, not just the routine.

A very similar thing also happens when I begin to pray privately in my devotional time. Likewise, I find that someone is already praying. The Holy Spirit is praying in me (Romans 8:26-27). Jesus is praying for me (Hebrews 7:24-25). The prayer meeting is already in session. We may even call it, reverently, a prayer duet. In this duet, there is oneness of purpose. There is harmony. There is contentment. There are words and rests. There is burden and direction. There is utter selflessness. Everything the Spirit and Son are praying is for the glory of God and the good of the Christian. There is never an exception to that goal. Knowing these things draws me. They settle me. I am coming to add my voice to the *same prayers*. I desire, by enabling grace, that the duet becomes a trio. I have to listen. There is both a rhythm and melody in prayer. What is even more wonderful is that the Father delights to hear my voice. He has designed prayer to include my voice. The trio is a sweet sound to His ears.

He intends to work through the prayers of His church. I personally believe that God has deliberately limited Himself. His self-imposed limits are that He has decided to work through prayer. Jesus said, "Up until now you have asked nothing in my name. Ask and you will receive, and your joy will be complete" (John 16:24). He has given us His name. We are to transact His business in His name. This is what *power of attorney* means. It is the legalized right to act in the name and on behalf of another. "In Jesus' name" is not, first of all, a signal that my prayer is over. It is a declaration that I have transacted His holy business on earth, according to His plans.

How indispensably vital is the ministry of the Holy Spirit to all this! That is why turning our emphasis to prayer is not a fundamental shift in the theme of this book, but an inevitable one. Jesus was in fact preeminently a man who prayed. This was His main ministry. Everything flowed from that. His intercessions for the church are the strength that holds the church together. Because of His prayers, the gates of hell are no match for the church. To be sure, the disciples were cloudy on a lot of things Jesus taught. But not on this one. It was crystal clear to them; what they saw/heard in Jesus was somehow connected to what they already knew He did the most— pray—hence, the request, "Lord, teach us to pray" (Luke 11:1). They understood innately that the praying life and the effective life are inseparable. The Holy Spirit is our gracious helper in all this. Jesus will teach us to pray through Him.

Let's consider first some fundamentals of prayer. Every discipline has fundamentals. Riding a bicycle involves the fundamentals of balance. All sports are built on basic fundamentals. These are changeless. These are basic. Every height achieved in every undertaking, every goal reached, every expertise refined, have all had one thing in common: the fundamentals. It is so also with our prayer. The Holy Spirit is pleased to teach us increasingly about prayer. Indeed, we should be praying differently now than we did ten years ago because of this. Still, regardless of how deeply the Holy Spirit may take us in this ministry of prayer, He will do so based on prayer fundamentals. Always.

FUNDAMENTAL PRINCIPLE

Prayer brings the mind of God into any given circumstance. True, prayer begins in heaven, not earth. God has a plan. His plan is changeless and comprehensive. His plan is eternal. He has a plan for every situation. This plan was in His mind before He made the world. As remarkable as this sounds, it is true. We are told plainly that He works everything in conformity with the purpose of His will (Ephesians 1:11). This should greatly encourage you. God has a plan for the very situation you are currently praying about. We see this principle in scripture. It was in the mind of Jesus to send the Holy Spirit. He said so to His disciples in John 14:16.

In other words, the Holy Spirit didn't come at Pentecost because of the praying disciples only. Pray, they did. And they waited (Acts 1:4, 7, 12-14). But the Holy Spirit came at Pentecost primarily in response to our Lord's prayer, "And *I* will ask the Father and He will give you another advocate to help you and be with you forever— the Spirit of Truth" (John 14:16-17). Therefore, as the disciples were praying in the upper room, they were praying about what the Father had on His mind: namely, the sending of the Holy Spirit. Having done so, the prayer was answered. It is the same with us. The mind of God is ascertained from the Word of God. The Bible is what God thinks, transcribed onto paper. The Bible speaks in precepts and principles. The precepts are the black and white of scripture— the clear commands, the plain teaching. No one ever has to pray about whether adultery is okay or not (although I'm sorry to say that some have twisted the truth to justify adultery as well as most other sins). No. The Bible is clear: "Thou shalt not."

Then, there are principles in scripture. Many things in life are not black and white. There is a lot of gray. Still, the scriptures speak. The Bible will never tell you which car to buy. That would be black and white. But the Bible does speak about wisdom, counsel, indebtedness, money management and financial priorities, and guidance in circumstances. God is at work in all of these dynamics, faithfully guiding His children into something utilitarian, yet so necessary even as buying a car. He has a plan even for that. This is why a good portion of my prayer time should be spent listening and not talking. The Holy Spirit will guide you. After spending time reading and meditating on the Word, He begins to prompt us. We sense His persuasion. His burden. His mind. We pray accordingly. Our praying may sound something like this: "Father, I see here your truth regarding the matter about which I'm praying. You seem to be speaking either by precept or principle to this very situation. I thank you and join my heart with yours for the accomplishment of your purpose."

When we think about this, we discover how very normal this is. A husband and wife share an intimate relationship. They share with one another the depths of their hearts. This is normal, natural, and to be expected. The church is the bride-elect of Jesus Christ. He is the groom. He is responsible for the church. The church is responsible to Him. He is the head. The church is the body. Indeed, our physical bodies cannot function apart from leadership and direction from the head. Everything our physical bodies do is because of nerve impulses and signals from our head. Jesus Christ is the Head of the church. We pray according to His mind. This is fundamental and never changes. I even envision myself in my daily praying as saying, "Here I am, Sir, reporting for duty." I do believe this is the right sequence. When I do this, the Holy Spirit will communicate to me the mind of God. He will do this to the extent I need to know it. In this way, He will get glory, and we will bear fruit (John 15:7-8).

FUNDAMENTAL PRIORITY

In an almost indescribable way, God the Father wants us to be with Him. This is accomplished when we pray. We are with Him by virtue of the Son's obedience and by the Spirit's calling. This is outstanding to the point of unbelievability to some. *God wants me to be with Him?* Yes, dear one. Dare to believe it. It is so. Prayer becomes the appropriation of that desire of the Father's heart.

The following is a poor illustration, but maybe it will help some. As a means of communicating with one another, we have phones, letters, emails, and texting (to name a few). It is a way for us to be with each other until we can, physically. We will be with the Father one day. We will be in His physical presence in a physical place. But until then, we may communicate, associate, talk, listen, and engage. This is prayer. This places child with father. This is the heart and desire of the Father.

We see this truth presented clearly in the Old Testament. The Lord walked with Adam and Eve in the Garden of Eden (Genesis 3:8). He was expressing His desire to be with them. This priority on God's part became more formalized many years later. Now no longer content to just walk with two, He desired to be with an entire nation and for that nation to be with Him. In giving Moses instructions for the tabernacle and the completion thereof, God said He would then dwell among them (Exodus 25:8). This dwelling was evidenced by the pillar of cloud and fire night and day (Exodus 13:21-22). It was particularly evidenced, however, at the tabernacle. This became the place of God's visible glory. His glory, in fact, filled the tabernacle, so much so that Moses wasn't ever able to minister (Exodus 40:34). How wonderful that would be if that happened every time the church met. Can you imagine your pastor standing up to preach but unable to do so because of the overwhelming glory of His presence?

God's glory is in fact His manifest presence. Every Christian has His presence by virtue of His in-dwelling Holy Spirit. Then, however, there are those times when He manifests Himself. Contrary to popular notions that suggest this sort of manifest presence of God would elicit all sorts of verbal, audible, and physical responses, I believe just the opposite would be true. Moses couldn't do anything. It seems almost like a holy paralysis. Indeed, there are those times when we are rightly reluctant to say or do anything, lest we grieve His holy presence. He is drawing near in those times. He's revealing Himself. It is fitting that we be silent. When God manifested Himself to Isaiah, the response was "Woe" from Isaiah (Isaiah 6:5). When the Lord manifested Himself to John on Patmos, John fell at His feet as though dead (Revelation 1:17). This sort of "awestruck" behavior has typified the response of God's people throughout scripture and history. We are long overdue for this in our own time and culture.

Wait on God. Long for Him. He certainly longs for you. He desires to manifest Himself to you. He did this at the tabernacle. Then some four hundred years later, God did this again. It was no longer at the tabernacle, which was temporary. It was at the temple that was a non-mobile, permanent structure. We see this in 2 Chronicles 5:13-14: "The temple was filled with the cloud, and the priests could not perform their service because of the cloud, for the glory of the Lord filled the temple of God." Again, can you even imagine this? The simple conclusion is that when the glorious presence of God is obvious, nothing else needs to be said or done.

We move ahead some four hundred more years. Now the story is a sad one. Ezekiel tells us that the glory of God departed the temple (Ezekiel 10:18). Oh, how tragic is this! A severe move on the part of our God. A heart-wrenching move for our God. Nonetheless, it was fully disclosed and prophesied by Him. The centuries of wooing, forgiving, and restoring had run their course. Israel was unbelievably stubborn and headstrong. The promised captivity was now upon them. They would now live in Babylon, no longer in glory.

Still, our God is gracious. A remnant returned to Jerusalem. After the seventy years, Zerubbabel, Ezra, and Nehemiah led three different companies of Israelites back to the city of David. The foundation, walls, and temple were eventually rebuilt. Life was resumed, but, the difference in pre-exilic and a post-exilic Israel was palpable. The "glory days" of David and Solomon were over. That dynamic will remain so until our Lord's return to the Holy City. At that time, the latter glory, which will be so much more than the former glory, will be revealed.

Back to our timeframe. The clock of history continued to wind down. The Old Testament era came to a close and so began the intertestamental years. Those years, again, were some four hundred in length. Imagine this: four hundred years and no manifest glory of God. Four hundred years and no word from God. Silence. It was during those years that the Pharisees had their beginnings. Remember? They were the nitpickers! They could not be satisfied. Critical, judgmental, and accusative. They had no glory of God! This will always be the case. Whenever I find myself acting the same way, it means that I've lost all sense of His glory. That's the time for me to get on my knees and wait. That's the time to ask Him for a fresh revelation of Himself.

Finally, however, this intertestamental period closed, and the New Testament opened. There, these words greet us: "The Word became flesh and made his dwelling among us. We have seen his glory, the glory of the one and only Son, who came from the Father, full of grace and truth" (John 1:14). This is outstanding. Can we even grasp it? The glory of God, His manifest presence—at the tabernacle and the temple and then withdrawn for hundreds of years—is now seen again . . . in His Son! The glory of God, residing in the Son of God! Every day for some thirty-three years, when people saw Jesus, they saw God!

This is simply overwhelming. Then, Jesus ascended after the Cross and Resurrection. Where now is His glory? His manifest presence? *In you*, dear one! This was Paul's incredible announcement to the church in Corinth (2 Corinthians 3:7-18; 4:7-12). *In you!* The Holy Spirit is indwelling you. He is the Spirit of glory. God the Father is manifesting Himself through you by the Person of the Holy Spirit, so that the Son will get glory. This is fundamental. God wants to be with us. To accomplish that, He indwells us by His Holy Spirit. When we pray, therefore, we are necessarily with Him, and He is with us. This is His plan and priority. He carries on His divine business through His church as she prays. This truth should overwhelmingly encourage you to pray. Then, don't forget, the logical conclusion is that people all around you also see His glory, His manifest presence through you. This is not burdensome. This is a delight. "So that the life of Jesus may be revealed in our body" (2 Corinthians 4:10).

A FUNDAMENTAL PRECEPT

A fundamental precept is this: We learn to pray by praying. Since you are now reading this book, are you not mindful that doing so would have been impossible when you were a baby? When you and I were babies, we learned to talk by listening and then saying what we heard. That led later on to sentences and grammar. The result is that we can now read. Prayer is the same way. We learn prayer language by listening and then saying what we've heard! We are listening to and for the Holy Spirit. He speaks primarily through the Bible. The Bible becomes our environment. Its truth directs our words in prayer. We learn to pray by praying. There are no experts, only learners. There are no degrees received in this school. No one ever graduates! While this school is always in session, there are those particular and necessary scheduled times for praying. This is indispensable. Jesus had His, and we must have ours (Mark 1:35). You must establish this time under the Holy Spirit's leadership.

Much has been made about early morning quiet time. This is certainly my personal schedule, but there is no insistence here. You may well set another time of day. The Holy Spirit will lead you. You must be deliberate, however, in your own sense of this quiet time being non-negotiable. You must not see it as a religious function to check off on a list. You must see it as life and the utter inability to live life without it. Holy God does meet with us. We do pray with expectation (Psalm 5:3). He does long to reveal Himself.

Not only should we set a beginning time, but we should also set a finishing time. Some are ambiguous at this point. They may conclude after even a few minutes, "I'm not getting anything out of this," and simply stop. Ask the Lord to guide you in establishing a quiet time. Should it be fifteen minutes? Thirty? Ninety? I don't know the answer for you, but the Lord will surely give clarity as you ask Him. Additionally, you will find your devotional times taking on their own personality. That is to say, the Holy Spirit will enable you to find your rhythm. What works for someone else may not necessarily work for you.

My own devotional times start early and include writing in a journal (I've kept one since 1978), writing down prayer requests and prayer answers, sometimes even writing out my prayers, systematic Bible reading, singing both from a hymnal and choruses, memorizing scripture, extended silence, usually a reading from a daily devotional book, and sometimes reading a few pages of theology. This has been honed out after several years and works well for me at this stage in life. I am certain, however, it will continue to change, as well it should. A growing relationship cannot remain static. That is just as true in our heavenly relationship as with our earthly ones.

A FUNDAMENTAL PURPOSE

All of this begs the question, *What is prayer's fundamental purpose?* Isn't the purpose of prayer to get answers? Certainly, answered prayer *is* one of the results of prayers rightly prayed. But, fundamentally, the purpose of prayer is that the glory due to the name and person of Jesus is acknowledged and recognized. This is precisely what our Lord taught in John 14:13: "And I will do whatever you ask in my name, so that the Father may be glorified in the Son." To say it another way: Whenever I pray for healing from sickness but am not healed, yet still somehow God gets glory, then, the fundamental purpose is achieved. The issue here for "non-healing" is seldom one of faith. It has been said that it takes more faith to stay sick when that's the will of God for you than to get well. This was the attitude of Jesus at the grave of Lazarus. Jesus deliberately waited until Lazarus was dead before He showed up (John 11:1-44). Certainly, God received greater glory from Jesus raising a dead man than He would have had Jesus merely healed a sick man.

This truth seems so hard for so many. Yet one of the most oft repeated promises in scripture is the promise of difficulty and tribulation. Paul was never healed from this thorn in the flesh. But did God get glory from Paul's life? I speak as a fool. A long range, eternal perspective, the big picture always, prescribes our Lord's dealings with us. In fact, He is positioning us for greater things in glory by demonstrating His glory now in our lives, which may seem to be so very hard indeed (2 Corinthians 4:16-18).

In answering prayer, God always takes the path whereby He will receive the greatest glory. This is at least part of what it means to pray in Jesus' name. Praying in Jesus' name is another way of saying, "I'm praying for Jesus to receive glory when and how He answers my prayer." This principle permeated even our Lord's own praying (John 17:1-26). Make no mistake, dear one. Be thoroughly encouraged. The Father will keep His promises to meet your every need. You can pray confidently, and our needs may be defined as whatever is necessary for God to achieve His will in and for our lives. The pathway to that realization will sometimes include the following: whatever the circumstances; in need; to have plenty; being content in any and every situation; whether well fed or hungry; living in plenty or in want; learning the ability to do all things through Him who gives strength (Philippians 4:11-13). When He gives the strength, He gets the glory. Praying this prayer is to always pray in the will of God.

Before I conclude this chapter on prayer, I want to include one final challenge and encouragement. I hope this will push you over the edge—take you to the next level. It is this: through prayer, the world is changed, and history is shaped. We see this pattern flawlessly repeated throughout the recorded prayers in scripture:

- Moses prayed, and a nation was saved (Exodus 32:1-14).

- Joshua prayed, and the sun stood still (Joshua 10:12).

- Elisha prayed, and his servant's eyes were opened to see the vast army of holy angels surrounding them (2 Kings 6:14-17).

- Nehemiah prayed, and the wall around Jerusalem was rebuilt (Nehemiah 1:4-11; 6:16).

- Daniel prayed, and Israel's future was communicated to him (Daniel 9:1-27).

- The church prayed, and Peter was released from prison (Acts 12:1-11).

- Our Lord prayed in Gethsemane, and victory was achieved at Calvary (Matthew 26:36-46).

In all of these examples—and dozens more in scripture—the world was changed, and history was shaped. I hope you will remember that the next time you get on your knees.

I recently noticed a book titled *One Thousand Events Which Shaped the World*. I feel fairly confident that prayer probably wasn't mentioned, yet we know the truth, don't we? It has pleased the Lord to ultimately position the church by His side for eternal ruling and reigning with Him. Until that day, the church even now does that through prayer. It is that which changes the world and shapes history.

CHAPTER 18

THE HOLY SPIRIT
AND SIN

Certainly, nothing offends us more rudely than this doctrine of original sin, and yet without this mystery, the most incomprehensible of all, we are incomprehensible to ourselves. (Blaise Pascal)

A Christian can know the joy of not sinning. Someone once said that victory is never sweeter than successfully withstanding temptation by the power and help of the Holy Spirit. A Christian can always look at temptation and say, "I can, but I don't have to." Whenever a Christian sins, he or she is believing and acting on a lie. Always. Satan is a deceiver, and so he deceives. This is his specialty. He somehow convinces the Christian that the forbidden fruit is not that big of a deal after all. Christians seem to buy into this. Since Jesus offers and promises forgiveness, it seems that some believers are casual rather than horror-struck by their own sin. A vicious cycle seems to characterize the entirety of the lives of some believers: sin, repent. It is the same sin over and over, not unlike Israel during the period of the judges. There is nothing of the Cross to resurrection victory here. Jesus didn't save us from sin only to have us keep on sinning. To believe so is to indeed embrace a perverted theology.

Am I talking about sinless perfectionism? No...and neither is the Bible. In fact, our brother John assures us that when we do sin (citing the possibility, not the pattern), we have an advocate who prays for us and who forgives us (1 John 1:8–2:1). Jesus says to the Father, "Put that on my account." What a marvelous and merciful Savior is this! So then, we may make a biblically sound statement regarding the Christian and sin. Namely, for the growing Christian, sin should be with decreasing frequency. This seems like news to some believers. In fact, it seems to never even be questioned. The logic is that Christians sin, and Jesus forgives. So why concern myself with not sinning? So the argument goes. To confront that sort of lazy, easy-believism, take for granted, you don't know my circumstances, spiritual pablum, I want to suggest six dynamics that take place simultaneously whenever a Christian sins. We may even call it the anatomy of sin.

Knowing the enemy is an incredible advantage in any battle. Sin is the enemy of the Christian. So whenever the Christian sins . . .

1. *We exhibit our sin nature.* I have heard of some Bible teachers who teach a one nature Christian. The new nature. The nature of Jesus Christ. This, to the exclusion of the sin nature. This rationale says the new nature is incapable of sinning. While Jesus never sinned—and never will—we are told plainly in scripture that there still resides within the Christian the sin nature, which is hostile to the Lord Jesus (Romans 6:18). This nature is not eradicated, as we've already tried to show in chapter thirteen. So whenever the Christian sins, they are making a willful choice. Please remember that. No one can make you sin. No, not even the devil. Every time I sin, it is because I've chosen to. When I do that, I am claiming a position that belongs to God alone. I have, in essence, become my own god. In truth, no one tells Holy God what to do. He is autonomous. He does as He pleases in the heavens and on the earth (Daniel 4).

   Whenever I sin, I am acting on my own. I am acting not dependent on but independent of God. This is not small nor to be dismissed. Sin is always active rebellion against God. It mocks the Cross and makes light of the blood. This should crush us. "See from His head, His hands, His feet; sorrow and love flow mingled down." This sin nature is haughty and powerful. Some, not realizing this, believe they can simply suppress it. It is no more possible to suppress the sin nature than it is to suppress an earthquake. No, the answer is in our appropriation of our own co-death/burial and resurrection with Jesus Christ. When I do that, the very indwelling life of Jesus not only hates the sin by which I'm tempted but gives me His power over it.

2. *We exchange the glory of God.* When a Christian sins, he or she is saying, "This (sin) is preferable to the glory of God." To fall short of the glory of God (Romans 3:23) is to prefer/prize something more than His glory.

    It has been said that whenever we seek less than the glory of God in all things, we, in fact, set in motion the disorder of all things. Adam and Eve's sin set in motion the disorder of all things. Our planet is diseased. Everyone on it has it. Sin kills. Its wages are death. Preferring anything over the glory of God says that I want what I see more than the One who makes what I see. When I sin, I have in fact chosen something that I want more than the glory of God. I "glory" in other things. Heartbreakingly, most of the world still takes the bait.

3. *We expose Jesus to sin.* Our Lord's commitment to us is that He will never leave us. Never. Not even when we sin. Whether that sin be in the heart or with the hand. In the mind or with the eye. In my words or in my steps. Jesus is there, watching, hearing, seeing. We expose Him to it. This is unthinkable and an extremely hard truth to hear. But, hear it we must. This could be likened to accompanying a war veteran back to a country where he fought for liberty and freedom. It would be to his shock, however, if he observed the residents of that country still living as if he'd never

come. Still living like they did when under an oppressive regime. The veteran might say, "So many of my fellow soldiers gave their lives for these people. Their blood is on the ground. Freedom was won! Yet these people are living as if nothing ever happened. It is too much for me to see. The exposure is more than I can bear."

Jesus gave His life for us. He liberated us from the oppressive regime of Satan. We must not go on living as if He had never come. We must not expose Him to that which would bring such grief to Him.

These three things happen every time we sin. They are things that happen on the earth. Yet simultaneous with that, three other things are happening. There is something going on in heaven. Jesus is faithful, and He watches over His sheep. Even when the Christian sins.

4. *There is intercession.* Jesus always prays for us. He never stops (Hebrews 7:25). This particular kind of praying is called intercession. It has been said that when we intercede, we are not first of all praying *for* someone as much as we are praying as that someone.15 It is a prayer of identity. Jesus identifies with us in our temptations (Matthew 4:1-10, Hebrews 4:15-16). Although at times we do tell Him how very hard and trying the temptation is, He nonetheless already knows. He stood immovable against the hottest blasts from hell. Satan threw everything at Jesus. Unsuccessfully. Jesus hasn't forgotten. He took every earthly experience back to heaven with Himself. Because He remembers and identifies, He intercedes. This is illustrated clearly in Luke 22:31-32. In this passage, we are taught that Satan must ask Jesus for permission for whatever he does. This must anger our enemy to no end. But he must live with it. He can't change it. He acts only with permission. Jesus tells Peter that Satan has demanded permission to sift all of them...plural (Luke 22:31) but that He has prayed for Peter...singular. Yes, Peter was the key to the rest and Satan knew it. Jesus then reassures Peter: ". . . but I have prayed for

---

15. Ron Dunn, *Don't Just Stand There, Pray Something* (Nashville: Thomas Nelson INC, 1992), 86.

you." The unspoken, but clearly understood assumption is, *Satan has asked permission, and I've given it.* Peter would be sifted. Indeed, needed to be. Peter was full of Peter. Jesus planned for him to be full of the Holy Spirit.

A principle comes to our attention from this story: in temptation, Satan's goal is to destroy; God's goal is to deepen. Peter was not destroyed. He was deepened. Jesus never stopped praying for Peter. Because of our Lord's intercession, Peter recovered from his sin and went on as an incredibly powerful instrument in our Lord's hands. We may accurately conclude from this vignette that the entirety of our lives is prayed over. Jesus prays us all the way home! Again, I can't say it too many times: Jesus never approves of our sin. He hates it. Always. His prayers are not approval but assurance. On these decreasing times, when I do sin, I am assured of His own plan for me remaining intact. Yes, I must respond. Going out and weeping bitterly as Peter did should characterize my every repenting. It is His very intercessions that enable me to do so.

5. *There is intervention.* Jesus, in the Person of the Holy Spirit, intervened in the church. We see this in Acts 5. Husband and wife team—Ananias and Sapphira—agreed together to lie against the Holy Spirit (Acts 5:3). It cost them their lives! Resulting from this was a great fear that seized the whole church (Acts 5:11). The Holy Spirit intervened and fostered holy fear on the rest of the church so that they would not give in to the same temptation.

When we are tempted to sin, we find in the Holy Spirit both our greatest ally as well as our greatest opponent. He hates sin. He fights against it. Always. Since sin is characteristic of my Adamic nature, I find myself fighting against God when I do sin (Romans 8:5-8). Even this is intervention that I might come to my senses and bow before His lordship in confession.

Many years ago, Billy Graham preached a sermon about how hard it is to get to hell. He said that "one would have to ignore a mother's prayers, a visiting/concerned pastor, an interceding church, the conviction of the Holy Spirit, and more." The conclusion, however, was that "Yes, sadly, one would finally make it to hell, but they would have to overcome all the obstacles and roadblocks God had put in the way." Similarly, a Christian may choose to sin. He will do so only by overcoming all the obstacles and roadblocks the Holy Spirit has placed in his way by virtue of intervention.

6. *There is invitation.* The smartest thing a tempted Christian can do is run to Jesus. He's the only one who can help us. As the song says, "No one understands like Jesus." He invites us to come to Him. Some may counter and say, "Since Jesus never sinned, how can He know about the agony of my own sin? How can He really understand?"

I once read the following illustration: You have a terminal disease and must choose between one of two surgeons. The first one says, "I've had this disease. I can help you." But can he really? It turns out that even though he's had your same disease, he's nonetheless never performed a surgery! The second surgeon says, "Although I've never had your disease, I have performed over nine hundred surgeries dealing with this very same disease. I know how it acts. I know what it does. I've encountered it and brought my expertise to bear upon it hundreds of times." Which surgeon would you choose? Silly question. Jesus has never had the disease of sin. Still, He is the expert. He's encountered it countless times. He dealt with it thoroughly on the Cross. He understands both its subtle nuances as well as its blatant demonstrations.

It flies in the very face of our sensibilities, then, to acknowledge that many Christians tend to run from, rather than run to, Jesus when they sin. Full of guilt or shame, they simply don't want to face Him. Remember dear one, no one ever knows you better—no one loves you more—than Jesus. He will not beat you up. Sin has already done that. He will rather dress your wounds and hold you closely to Himself. He knows why you sinned even if you don't. He will teach you! Increasingly, you will find in sin utter dissatisfaction, even nausea, and you will find in Him more—much more—than you ever found in what Augustine called "fruitless joys." Come to Jesus when you sin. Run to Jesus. Get there as fast as you can. His arms are open, and He is waiting, and in His arms, He carries His sheep, wounded by their own sin. He forgives, heals, instructs, and restores. He makes sure they are strong in the Spirit before He returns them to the battle.

Dear one, I hope you will hate sin. I hope it breaks your heart. I hope you will run from it. When all of this fails, however, and then you fail, look to Jesus. Go to Jesus. And even if you're so beaten by your sin and can't seem to do any of this, then don't despair; Jesus is coming to you! He will not abandon you. He will not leave you in your sin. He always has—and always will—go after His sheep.

The Ninety and Nine

There were ninety and nine that safely lay
In the shelter of the fold;
But one was out on the hills away,
Far off from the gates of gold.
Away on the mountains wild and bare;
Away from the tender Shepherd's care.

"Lord, Thou hast here Thy ninety and nine;
Are they not enough for Thee?"
But the Shepherd made answer
"This is Mine
Has wandered away from Me.
And although the road be rough and steep,
I go to the desert to find My sheep."

But none of the ransomed ever knew
How deep were the waters crossed;
Nor how dark was the night the Lord passed through
Ere He found His sheep that was lost.
Out in the desert He heard its cry;
'Twas sick and helpless and ready to die

"Lord, whence are those blood-drops all the way,
That mark out the mountain's track?"
"They were shed for one who had gone astray
Ere the Shepherd could bring him back."
"Lord, whence are Thy hands so rent and torn?"
"They're pierced tonight by many a thorn."

And all through the mountains, thunder-riv'n,
And up from the rocky steep,
There arose a glad cry to the gate of heav'n,
"Rejoice! I have found My sheep!"
And the angels echoed around the throne,
"Rejoice, for the Lord brings back His own!"[16]

---

16. Andrew Peterson (Public Domain).

CHAPTER 19

THE HOLY SPIRIT AND INTIMACY

In nature, everything moves in the direction of its hungers. In the spiritual world, it is not otherwise. We gravitate toward our inward longing, provided of course, that those longings are strong enough to move us. (A. W. Tozer)

Frankly, it is overwhelming. Holy, infinite, and eternal God, who needs nothing, deeply desires our intimacy. To this end, He made the first move. "For God so loved the world, that He gave His only begotten Son." That's the first move. The initiative. We can never know God, either initially at conversion or intimately through spiritual growth, apart from Jesus Christ and the Holy Spirit. God wants intimacy. He has said, "The Lord confides in those who fear Him; He makes His covenant known to them" (Psalm 25:14).

While it is true that God has no favorites, it is equally true that He does have intimates. He has also said, "Shall I hide from Abraham what I'm about to do?" (Genesis 18:18). Answer? No. He would not hide but would confide. Abraham was His friend (James 2:23), and true friends share at a deep level. This is the sort of relationship the Holy Spirit always presses toward. I believe that *everything*, in fact, the Father does, permits, allows, or prevents is for the purpose of fostering intimacy with Himself. This, indeed, is the qualifier in Romans 8:28: He works all things together for good for those who love Him. Love demonstrates a relationship of unshakable confidence and trust. This was unquestionably Paul's attitude in life. He said quite simply, "I want to know Christ" (Philippians 3:10). The word he uses for "know" is descriptive of the husband and wife intimacy.

How, then, does this sort of intimacy come about? Wouldn't you agree that there must be a foundation for such intimacy? That is, intimacy doesn't just happen. It is the result of *something*.

ABANDONMENT OF PREOCCUPATIONS

Earlier in Philippians 3, Paul lets us in on how this foundation of intimacy is built. These preoccupations are listed in verses 1-7 and could be categorized as (1) non-essentials, (2) heredity, and (3) achievements. Let's look at these separately.

Paul stated there are some non-essentials to salvation. Certainly, if they are non-essential for salvation, then they are completely inconsequential for intimacy. He lists these as circumcision (Philippians 3:1-3), legalism (by obvious implication), and righteousness, which comes from the law (Philippians 3:9). None of these things were or are necessary for salvation. Still, there was some insisting on those very things (Philippians 3:2). It is not much different in our own time. It seems all denominations have their lists. Sometimes those lists are surreptitious (nonetheless understood). Other lists are obvious and required. I think it boils down to what we're willing to fight for.

Those who fight over the color of the carpet in church have probably never known intimacy with Jesus. Rather, they are more intimate with their lists. Those who hold their peace and only fight when the name and honor of Jesus are at stake probably do have intimacy with Him. Jesus fought when His Father's house of prayer was turned into a den of thieves. The honor, glory, presence, pleasure, purpose, and smile of God are dynamics we must never abandon. Yet, there are some things we must abandon. We will only know God in an elementary, perfunctory way until we do. Paul wanted intimacy. To gain that, he gladly abandoned the non-essentials. Are there any in your life? Ask the Holy Spirit. He's the only one who knows for sure.

Then, what a pedigree Paul had (Philippians 3:4-6). Downright impressive! To have had his heredity would have pleased any non-messianic Jew. But again, Paul recognizes that while his credentials are impeccable—even enviable—nonetheless, they have nothing to do with salvation or intimacy. In that regard, they must be abandoned. This particular step is very hard for those who were reared in Bible believing, evangelical homes. It is hard to come to the place where we say, "What I'm now learning, the Bible teaches is different from this or that point I was taught growing up." We always give the benefit of the doubt. We believe that our forefathers were sincere and walked in the light they had. Yet no one understands all the truth. To the degree a Christian seeks God and the teaching of the Holy Spirit is the same degree to which he may expect revelation. Not new revelation—rather, increasing light on the old revelation. Still, it is hard. And yes, still it must be abandoned at whatever point the Holy Spirit instructs.

But Paul isn't finished yet. He concludes his abandonment trilogy with this coup de grace: "But whatever was gain to me, I now consider loss for the sake of Christ" (Philippians 3:7). A huge statement for a pragmatic, goal-oriented, objective-driven personality. Achievements! It is as if He wants us to say, "And, oh yes, just in case I've forgotten anything, I want to say everything. That makes it conclusive." Growing Christians become increasingly weary of everything not essentially connected to Jesus Christ. They are fatigued by the stuff, subterfuge, and sensationalism often associated with the Christian faith in western culture. Their hearts hunger for the simple and yet profound preacher of Galilee.

To hear Him is their delight. To please Him is their aim. To present Him is their ceaseless activity. They are radical and extreme in the purest sense of the words. They've been there and done that and found them gnawingly empty. "Just give me Jesus" is their hearts' cry. They are willing to abandon everything to have that cry satisfied. The foundation for intimacy necessitates an abandonment of preoccupations.

ABSORPTION BY A PERSON

This person is the Holy Spirit. This is the theme of this entire book. Paul doesn't mention Him by name, yet His activity is inescapable. It is He who directs our worship to and of Jesus Christ, who boasts only in Christ Jesus, and who puts no confidence in the flesh (Philippians 3:3). We may use the terms *absorbed by* and *filled with* the Holy Spirit synonymously. To be filled with Him is to be absorbed by Him. To be absorbed by Him is to be filled with Him. This absorption/filling, then, is tied inextricably with living in the truth or the Bible. Already mentioned earlier in the book, it bears comment again: I am never more filled with the Spirit than I am with the Word. This dynamic is never an either/or in scripture but a both/and. A spirit filled person—a person absorbed by the Holy Spirit—is a Word person. Plain and simple. When we take this truth and apply it in context to Philippians 3, we discover this Holy Spirit fullness/absorption results in a clear, biblical theology.

To say it another way, a person who traffics in preoccupations or is controlled by non-essentials, heredity, and achievements, does so because they either don't know or aren't growing in a biblical theology. They're living in eisegesis not exegesis (remember in chapter four?). One cannot grow in intimacy with Jesus Christ apart from a growing biblical theology revealing Him. If my perception of Jesus is not supported by biblical truth, then I am prey to any/all other perceptions. This leads to spiritual stagnation at the least and heresy at the worst. To put it another way still: I cannot know the Christ of scripture intimately without knowing the scripture of Christ. Paul, thus, lays a foundation for intimacy with Jesus Christ. He then takes the obvious next step and talks about a futility that exists without intimacy. Oh, how he underscores this abject emptiness apart from Jesus!

In Philippians 3:8 he uses a word that has multiple translations. The NIV reads, "What is more." Applying several accurate translations, this verse could read, "But, indeed, therefore, in fact, also, I consider everything a loss [Philippians 3:8] and dung [Philippians 3:9] when compared to knowing Christ Jesus." What a mouthful for a former religionist! At one time, in his former pharisaism, he had all the answers but no life. Now he has life because he also has intimacy.

The word *consider* in Philippians 3:8 is an accounting term. It also means to place before one's mind. We can imagine Paul mentally lining up the columns in his mind. Column one: his achievements. Column two: how these stack up when compared to intimacy with Jesus. Paul concludes: No contest! Futility.

What would you conclude about your own life? Is there anything you treasure more than Jesus? I feel certain we cannot answer that question apart from the Holy Spirit. Would you ask Him, *Holy Spirit, do I treasure anything more than Jesus?* He knows that treasuring Jesus is the very best thing for you. He will gladly show you if it isn't so, and He will show you how to make it so. Count Zinzendorf, founder of the Moravian Brethren, said, "I have but one passion. It is He!" May the same thing be so for us. Holy God desires intimacy with us. It is not flirty, casual, carnal, or flippant. It is, as Augustine said, like this: "You have made us for yourself, and our hearts are restless until they find rest in thee." Knowing God intimately through His Son, Jesus Christ, is the privilege and possibility for every Christian. Whosoever will, may come. Will you?

Perhaps the need that underlies all needs is that we are not hungry enough, not thirsty enough, not whole-souled enough in our desire. (Wesley Duewel)

CHAPTER 20

THE HOLY SPIRIT AND SUFFERING

Every affliction comes with a message from the heart of God! (Alexander Maclaren)

P aul's words must have stunned the Philippians: "I want to know Christ—yes, to know the power of his resurrection and participation in his sufferings" (Philippians 3:10). Then, as if that were not enough, Paul insists on "becoming like Him in His death." These words do not come from the mouth of a sadist, wishing for self-imposed martyrdom. Nor is he mentally unbalanced. He rather speaks as a Spirit-filled man, outlining what is intended to be the norm for every biblical Christian. Yes, the norm. Suffering is normal for the Christian. Indeed, Paul has already said that suffering was a gift (Philippians 1:29).

The sufferings of Jesus Christ refer to His Cross. The ignominy of that event was still fresh in the minds of so many. Less than thirty years had passed since the Crucifixion, yet Paul can't get away from it. Nor should we. He references it time and time again in his epistles. The Cross was the central event in history. The zenith. The apex. All of Old Testament looked forward to it. All of the New Testament looks back to it. Jesus Christ came to die for the sins of the world. In so doing, He took everyone else's place. He took your place on the Cross. I hope you understand this. You deserved to die. So did I. The mocking, humiliation, shame, and torture should have been felt and experienced by you. You and I should have been spat upon, ripped of our clothing, slapped in the face, bruised with fists, lacerated on our backs, and pierced in our hands and feet. But, even if all of this had happened to us, it would have accomplished absolutely nothing! Sinners can't justify sinners. Only Jesus can do that, and He did it on the Cross. It is this Cross that consumes Paul's mind. He understands there is not one way for Jesus and another way for us. No, we'll probably never be nailed to a cross, but sufferings that come to us because we are followers of Jesus are inseparable—in some way—from His sufferings on the Cross. How so?

The Cross is the only means for intimacy. Because Jesus died, the way is open for intimacy with God the Father through the ministry of the Holy Spirit. The Holy Spirit takes everything Jesus did for us and makes it reachable by us. Had there been no Cross, we would still be fixed in an Old Testament economy. The Cross is the only means to intimacy. The paradox is that it can also be the main interruption to intimacy. Sooner or later in our fellowship of Jesus, He will require that we do something. It will be out of our comfort zone. It will require more than ever before. It will be costly. Some may look at that next level required by the Lord and say, "No...that's too much for me. I can't humble myself and go to that person. I can't give this thing up. I can't go to another country. No. It requires too much. It is too inconvenient." What has just happened? Intimacy has been broken. The cost of following has been calculated to be too high, and the more comfortable road has been chosen. Jesus, however, is the perfect shepherd. He never confronts us with the next level until He knows we're ready. Going to the Cross was a thirty-three-year journey even for Him! But the time came, and He acted in perfect obedience. It is a paradox, isn't it?

The Cross is the only means to intimacy and can be the main interruption to intimacy. Paul treasured intimacy with Jesus Christ. He undertook every suffering necessary to maintain it (2 Corinthians 1:1-11; 4:7-13; 11:23-29). Intimacy results from obedience. A pastor said to me one time, "Always obey the Lord…no matter what…and leave the results to Him." I can't say it any better. This is what the Cross is about.

But, there is more. There is also a principle regarding the Cross and suffering. The principle is this: participation in one phase of our Lord's life positions me for greater intimacy, which then positions me to participate in the next phase. Or, if a Christian finds it difficult to participate in the Cross (which was the ultimate in our Lord's life), it may be that Christian has never participated in humility (which was basic in our Lord's life). Humble people carry their cross. Humble people stay on the cross.

We discussed this at some length in chapter thirteen. Referencing Romans 6, we simply consider two truths here, which give us insight regarding how to participate in our Lord's life. One is acknowledgment. Romans 6 is true. I don't have to feel it or have emotions about it. No adverse or favorable circumstances have to affirm it. But, I do have to acknowledge it. Did you know that you are as dead as anyone in any cemetery? Go to any cemetery and stand over any grave. Talk to the occupant. Fuss at that occupant. Praise that occupant. Blame that occupant. Do it every day…all day…for one hundred days. Do you know what that occupant will do? Absolutely nothing. They are dead. So are you. You died with Christ. That is a fact that nothing can ever change, and it is true whether or not you acknowledge it. But if you acknowledge it, then you can participate in His life. There's no participation in His life apart from participation in His death.

Yet even acknowledgement isn't enough. Appropriation must follow acknowledgement. When I appropriate something, I make that something mine. When I go shopping and take something off the shelf and pay for it, I am appropriating it. I make it mine. Everything Jesus died to give us must be appropriated by us, otherwise it just remains on the shelf. It is true that the Christian doesn't really have any needs. The Christian has Jesus and, therefore, has everything. But, the Christian does need to appropriate everything that they already have. Participation in the life of Jesus requires acknowledgement and appropriation. As another author said, "Jesus didn't die just to get us into heaven but to get Himself into us."[17]

---

17. Major W. Ian Thomas, *The Indwelling Life of Christ* (Colorado Springs: Multnomah Books, 2006), 54.

All of this does, however, lead somewhere. Suffering for the Christian is never arbitrary. It is never incidental or coincidental. There are purposes regarding the Cross and suffering. One of the purposes is mutuality. Mutuality simply says that He suffers with us still! John Stott observes that the early church fathers did not want to admit this. They seemingly couldn't accept the fact that the ascended Savior could in any way still suffer.[18] This was called the impassability of God. Impassability meant God is incapable of suffering. How the Cross smashes that idea into dust! God was in Christ, reconciling the world (2 Corinthians 5:19).

Jesus asked Saul, "Why are you persecuting Me" (Acts 9:4). As you know, Jesus was already in heaven at this time. Yet, how was He persecuted? His bride—His church—was being persecuted. Jesus was not aloof from, nor passive about, that. He suffered with His bride in that day. He suffers with her in our day. Think about it this way; A shepherd tending his sheep experiences the same things the sheep do: in rain, he gets wet; in low temperatures, he gets cold; in heat, he is hot; in drought, he is thirsty. I can't explain to you logically how Jesus suffers with us. I only know that He does. He does indwell us by the Holy Spirit, doesn't He? Therefore, He is exposed to everything we are. When someone abuses us, He is abused. When we grieve, He grieves with us. When we agonize with the lost, feel the blunt force of rejection and criticism, or endure the interminable lonely hours, Jesus is present and identifies with us. In fact, nothing can keep Him away. I hope you believe that. Please let the words of this song sink deeply into your heart. How very healing they are:

Does Jesus Care

Does Jesus care when my heart is pained
Too deeply for mirth or song,
As the burdens press,
And the cares distress,
And the way grows weary and long?

---

18. John R.W. Stott, *The Cross of Christ* (Downers Grove, IL: InterVarsity Press, 1986), 330–331.

Chorus:

O yes, He cares, I know He cares,
His heart is touched with my grief;
When the days are weary,
The long night dreary,
I know my Savior cares.

Does Jesus care when my way is dark
With a nameless dread and fear?
As the daylight fades
Into deep night shades
Does He care enough to be near?

(Chorus)

Does Jesus care when I've tried and failed
To resist some temptation strong;
When for my deep grief
There is no relief,
Though my tears flow all the night long?

Does Jesus care when I've said "goodbye"
To the dearest on earth to me
And my sad heart aches
Till it nearly breaks,
Is it aught to Him? Does He see?

(Chorus)

O yes, He cares, I know He cares,
His heart is touched with my grief;
When the days are weary,
The long night dreary,
I know my Savior cares.[19]

---

19. Frank E. Graeff, 1901 (Public Domain).

While Jesus can always say, "I know just how you feel," we can't always say, "I know just how *you* feel." This is the other side of mutuality. To participate in His sufferings is to be treated like He was. These sufferings come to us specifically because we are following Him. This means when we are ignored, not welcomed, misunderstood, and more-precisely, because of our fellowship of Jesus, we are sharing in a mutuality. This explains partially what Paul meant by these words to the church of Colossae: "Now I rejoice in what I am suffering for you, and I fill up in my flesh what is still lacking in regard to Christ's afflictions. For the sake of His body, which is the Church" (Colossians 1:24). Nothing, of course, was lacking in the atonement. Our Lord's words, "It is finished," mean just that. But there is a cost in following Jesus. He said that whenever people insult and persecute us and falsely say all manner of evil against us because of Him, we are to rejoice and be glad because of our great reward in heaven (Matthew 5:11). Every time these things happen to us because of Him, we may, then, say quietly in our hearts, "Yes, Lord Jesus. Thank you. I understand and know you a little bit better now. I know a little bit more about how indeed you feel." This is the idea of mutuality. It is one of His purposes in our suffering.

There is also the purpose of maturity. It has been said, "I've never known anyone God ever used significantly who didn't suffer deeply."[20] I agree with that. Scripture and church history agree with that. Mark it down; there is no Christian maturity apart from suffering. Suffering presses the point: *Why am I following Jesus? Will I continue following Him? What if He never rights the wrongs in my life? What am I expecting of Jesus?*

There is an easy Christianity in our western culture. We know essentially nothing of suffering. And that which costs us nothing usually means nothing. We get offended at God if He doesn't heal our big toe! All the while, our brothers and sisters internationally are being raped, dismembered, and killed.

I tremble because, "to whom much has been given, much will be required." Christians in America have been given more than any other generation of Christians. Much is, and will be, required of

---

20. Charles R. Swindoll, *Killing Giants, Pulling Thorns* (Portland: Multnomah Press, 1978), 40.

us. Still, suffering is necessary for maturity. It sounds strange to us, but it is true: God is doing us a favor when He permits suffering in our lives. The gold must be purified. The dross must be burned away. The most mature Christian you know has suffered. There is never an exception to that. Even Jesus was made perfect through suffering (Hebrews 2:16). Though already perfect, it was through His obedient suffering that He demonstrated that. The psalmist said, "Before I was afflicted I went astray, but now I obey your word" (Psalm 119:67), and, "It was good for me to be afflicted so that I might learn your decrees" (Psalm 119:71).

Enduring the shame and reproach of the Cross was the ultimate for Jesus. It is the same for us. The one who endures the cross can endure anything. Paul was willing to suffer. All who live godly in Christ Jesus will. But surely, intimacy is worth it, don't you think? Or do you? I hope you will answer that question.

> It is not what enemies will, nor what they are resolved upon, but what God will, and what God appoints, that shall be done. And as no enemy can bring suffering upon a man when the will of God is otherwise, so no man can save himself out of their hands when God will deliver him up for His Glory. We shall or shall not suffer, even as it pleaseth Him. God has appointed who shall suffer. Suffering comes not by chance or by the will of man, but by the will and appointment of God. (John Bunyan)

CHAPTER 21

IMMANENCE AND TRANSCENDENCE

Be sure to distinguish between the fact of God's presence and the feeling of the fact. It is actually a wonderful thing when our soul feels lonely and deserted, as long as our faith can say, "I do not see You, Lord, nor do I feel Your presence, but I know for certain You are graciously here—exactly where I am and aware of my circumstances." Remind yourself again and again with these words: "Lord, You are here. And though the bush before me does not seem to burn, it does burn. I will take the shoes from my feet, for the place where (I am) standing is holy ground" (Exodus 3:5).
(London Christian)

In the city where I was born, there stands a beautiful church. Once a week my grandparents, with whom I lived in the country, would drive into the city. The purpose of that trip was to pay the bills (always by cash) and to eat at the S&W Cafeteria. We always parked on Church Street. Appropriately named because of the many churches that lined it. But I was drawn to a particular church. To *that church.* What drew me? The large wooden and iron doors? The incredibly beautiful architecture? The sovereign hand of God teaching me a lesson I would still remember many decades later? The answer is yes to all the previous questions, superintended by the last. There was no question. I was drawn to that church. While my grandparents were moving purposefully along, I seized any opportunity to make my dash! As soon as I opened the door, there it was. I saw it. An enormous stained-glass window. All that stood between it and me were the pulpit, choir loft, and pews. There I stood, by myself. Absorbing. Consuming. Mentally inhaling.

Something was going on inside of me. It was neither hype nor hysteria. To the contrary, that transfixed moment felt good, stabilizing, and right. After staring at that beautiful stained glass for a few moments, I dashed off again to rejoin my grandparents. So what *was* going on inside of me? I didn't know it then (but do now) that God was tugging at the heart of a little boy. He was revealing Himself to me. I had just entered theological kindergarten. The subject was the transcendence of God. Transcendence is simply defined by Webster as "surpassing, excelling, extraordinary." Theologians use the word in tandem with immanence: transcendence and immanence. Immanence describes God's person and activity within His creation. He is at work in and through the natural processes (Millard J. Erikson, *Introducing Christian Doctrine*, second edition, page 87). Immanence is another way of expressing God's "omnis": He is *omni*present (everywhere), *omni*potent (all powerful), and *omni*scient (all knowing).

God is at work in culture, history, governments, hospitals, and families. He is at work in the godless as well as the godly. He is immanent in His creation. No one or no thing is ultimately truant from His perfect supervision. God is present. God is here. This is my Father's world. He is the God who is immanent. But He is also and equally transcendent. He is not only present in our world, He is present and beyond our world. He is other-worldly. His transcendence takes us beyond His immanence. He is above. He is other. He has no limitations or termination. He is not bound by time or space. Because of this, Moses hid his face (Exodus 3:7), Isaiah cried, "Woe is me" (Isaiah 6:5), Peter said, "Get away from me...I am a sinful man" (Luke 5:8). To these men, God was present (immanent). And He was beyond (transcendent).

The Holy Spirit is the one who quickens us to each of these dynamics. Our relationship with the Father, through the Son, enlightened by the Spirit, includes immanence and transcendence. And how we need the Holy Spirit's help! For example, some believers seem to never think of the very present Lord Jesus. There seems to be nothing about them that indicates they are thinking of Him. He is not immanent to them. Very much less is He transcendent to them. The Holy Spirit is always working on behalf of the father/child, chief shepherd/sheep relationship. He wants us to know increasingly our immanent and transcendent God. However, there is the possibility of extremism. There are believers who take immanence beyond the biblical standards. They want their present, active God to think and act as they do. They want a pragmatic black and white God. They want answers to every question. They want a God they can manage and control.

This position moves so subtly into idolatry. It tries to make God in my image. To this Christian, God is ordinary, casual, and exists to serve them. They're not satisfied with the secret things belonging to God (Deuteronomy 29:29). At this point, the securing and reassuring doctrine of immanence succumbs to the perfunctory. There is no awe of God. He is no longer breathtaking.

On the other hand, there are those who seem to only prefer the transcendence of God. They are also susceptible to extremes. They also go beyond the biblical parameters. For this Christian, if everything isn't always sensational and unexplainable, then God isn't in it. In other words, to them God is more of a performer than a person. They want an experience more than a relationship. Instead of a beautiful leaf falling to the ground (God immanent in nature), they want a leaf falling to the ground to mean something mysterious and supernatural (transcendent). Nonetheless, God is both, and the Holy Spirit teaches us both.

Let's consider then the power of the Holy Spirit demonstrated in our lives as we live in the immanence of God. Let me put it another way: very few would associate the fullness of the Holy Spirit in the "everyday-ness" of life. Washing the clothes, paying the bills, changing the diapers, dusting the furniture, etc. Everyday-ness. Think about Moses, David, and John the Baptist. Think of the years they all spent in the everyday-ness of the wilderness, tending sheep and eating locusts and wild honey. Holy Spirit fullness? Most would say "no." Unfortunately, they would counter, "crossing the Red Sea," "slaying Goliath," "announcing the Lamb of God who takes away the sin of the world!" Now, that's fullness! But it begs a question, doesn't it? How can a few mountaintop experiences demonstrate fullness when the years of preparation necessary for those demonstrations don't? I rest my case. Was there even one moment in the thirty or so years of our Lord's life when He was not full of the Holy Spirit? No. Not even one moment. Three years followed of the unprecedented: the miraculous God in the flesh. Was not Paul full of the Holy Spirit all during his incredible trials and hostile treatment (2 Corinthians 1:1-11; 11:23-29)? And so, the list goes on both in church and biblical history. There are no exceptions. We can't even do "whatever we do as unto the Lord" (Colossians 3:17) without the fullness of the Holy Spirit. Fullness is Jesus living in you, every day, powerfully and calmly. As Elizabeth Elliot said, "The answer is not a different set of circumstances, but Jesus in you, adequate for all circumstances!"[21] The Christian may know His fullness in the everyday-ness of life.

This is a great promise, but then there is the transcendence of God. In His immanence, He is present. In His transcendence, He manifests His presence. For example, if you or I were driving down the highway with our mate, we would have their presence. Two people in one car. Together. Present. But whenever we start talking, fellowshipping, or holding hands, we then have manifest presence. There's an engagement, awareness, connection.

This is what happens in transcendence. Holy God may "step in" at any time. He manifests Himself. It may happen in a worship service or when you're washing your car! Suddenly you're aware, "God is here!" The natural gives way to the supernatural. The ordinary to the extraordinary. No definition is adequate here. No explanation fully possible.

The story is told of the 1949 New Hebrides Islands Revival. Duncan Campbell was the preacher. After a very normal worship service had concluded, the congregation was dismissed. While moving from the church to the surrounding roads and paths, Campbell suddenly heard a church elder say, "Stand, Mr. Campbell, God has come! God has come! See what is happening!" Recounting this story, Campbell said, "And I looked toward the congregation,

---

21. Elizabeth Elliot, *Keep A Quiet Heart* (Ann Arbor, MI: Vine Books Servant Publications, 1995), 20.

and I saw them falling on their knees among the heather. I heard the cries of the penitent. And that meeting that began at 11:00 that night continued on the hillside until 4:00 in the morning" (Duncan Campbell, *The Nature of God-Sent Revival*). This is transcendence. This is a great promise.

It is not anything we work up. It is God manifesting Himself among His people. Does this sound wonderful to you? I hope so. Still, there are those who are very uncomfortable with this. They don't know how to stop and wait. They don't know how to not sing an ordered hymn in the order of worship. They are restless with silence and afraid of the un-programmed. And they miss God; yet, no one has to. God is not a science. He does not fit into any neat formula. The Spirit blows where He will. Our part is the willingness to go into the unknown (Abraham went out not knowing where he was going). We must do the same. I call this seeing the invisible, hearing the inaudible, believing the impossible.

I hope you will live in the power of the Holy Spirit in the everyday-ness of life. I hope you will live in the power of the Holy Spirit when God breaks into the everyday-ness. He is immanent. He is transcendent. The Holy Spirit desires—and will help us—to live fully in both.

CHAPTER 22

NOW WHAT; SO WHAT?

The man who aims at nothing hits it. (Daniel O'Connell)

I've been in church all my life. My parents saw to that, and because of that, I feel hugely fortunate and blessed. *(Thanks, Mom and Dad)*. In all of those growing up years, while sitting, listening to the preacher, I never once doubted what he was saying. No...not even once. I did, however, leave those worship services thinking, *Now what; so what?* This is a good question. Or we could say, "Revelation without application is stagnation." It matters critically how we hear (Matthew 13:1-23). And it matters critically what we do with what we hear. The Lord does hold us accountable for what we do with His truth.

I hope you have resonated with what I've said in these pages. I would be shocked if you agreed with all of it and would probably even raise a question about your honesty! No. What you do now with what you've read is between you and the Holy Spirit. You already know that I believe in sovereignty. Because of that, I regard it as no accident that you've read this book. I encourage you to do what I ask my congregation to do at the close of every worship service: Ask the question, *Lord, what are You saying to me?* Would you ask Him to do that for you regarding this book? Please, be as specific as possible. Write it down. Try and put it into words. Perhaps pose some questions:

- Is there something I need to do?
- Have I learned something?
- Where have I agreed with the writer?
- Where have I disagreed?
- Do I need to follow up with further study?
- What would I say is the central theme of this book?
- Has my worship been affected?
- Has my relationship with the Lord been affected?

My point is this: Please make some deliberate application. Please answer the question, *Now what; so what?*

Frankly, there's more I want to say. My relationship with the Holy Spirit is, by grace, growing. I am learning more about our great Savior Jesus. And that's the way it should be for all of us. Yet every book must have a stopping place as surely as a starting place. So this will be mine with this prayer for you: if the Holy Spirit has been a stranger to you, I hope by now He has become your friend and that you will significantly deepen your affection for Him as He shows Jesus to you more and more until we are called home.

PARTING WORD

I was ordained to the Gospel Ministry in 1980. At that service, my dad played an incredible piano solo. These were the words behind the music:

Come Holy Spirit

The Holy Spirit came at Pentecost,
He came to mighty fullness then;
His witness thru believers won the lost,
And multitudes were born again.

The early Christians scattered o'er the world,
They preached the Gospel fearlessly;
Tho' some were martyred and to lions hurled,
They marched along in victory!

Come, Holy Spirt,
Dark is the hour,
We need your filling,
Your love and your mighty pow'r
Move now among us,
Stir us, we pray.
Come, Holy Spirt,
Revive the church today!

Then in an age when darkness gripped the earth,
"The just shall live by faith" was learned;
The Holy Spirit gave the Church new birth
As reformation fires burned.
In later years the great revivals came,
When saints would seek the Lord and pray;
O, once again we need that holy flame
To meet the challenge of today!

Come, Holy Spirt,
Dark is the hour,
We need your filling,
Your love and your mighty pow'r
Move now among us,
Stir us, we pray.
Come, Holy Spirit,
Revive the church today! [22]

---

22. John W. Peterson, "Come, Holy Spirit" (1971).

CPSIA information can be obtained
at www.ICGtesting.com
Printed in the USA
FFOW03n2322220618
47210296-49984FF